The Chump Lady Survival Guide to Infidelity

How to Regain Your Sanity After You've Been Cheated On

The Chump Lady Survival Guide to Infidelity

How to Regain Your Sanity After You've Been Cheated On

By Tracy Schorn

Copyright © 2014 by Tracy Schorn

All rights reserved. No part of this publication may be reproduced, distributed, or transmitted in any form or by any means, including photocopying, recording, or other electronic or mechanical methods, without the prior written permission of the publisher, except in the case of brief quotations embodied in critical reviews and certain other noncommercial uses permitted by copyright law. For permission requests, write to the publisher, addressed "Attention: Permissions," at the address below.

Chump Lady Permissions
103 E. San Antonio St.
Lockhart, Texas
78644
www.chumplady.com
info@chumplady.com

Printed in the United States of America

First Printing, 2014

ISBN-13:978-1493554003
ISBN-10:149355400X

Library of Congress Control Number: 2014911144
CreateSpace Independent Publishing Platform, North Charleston, SC

"I prayed for twenty years but received no answer until I prayed with my legs."

—*Frederick Douglass*

Acknowledgments

I'd like to acknowledge Chump Nation. I knew you were out there, I just had no idea how mighty you were until I started my blog. Thank you for making Chump Lady a vibrant, compassionate community of fellow chumps.

Thank you to every anonymous chump online who pulled me out of the abyss when I experienced infidelity. Every day I try to pay it forward because of your kindness.

Thank you to Yoma. You financed the liberation campaign and were the best friend anyone could ever have. You taught me the calming power of the 3 a.m. bowl of raisin bran.

Thanks, Jenn, for the talks over breakfast tacos. Some day we'll get in shape. Until then… pumpkin muffins.

Thanks to my family. Especially my parents, to my mother who can sniff out bullshit and has never had a filter. The unvarnished straight talk comes from your side. And to my father for always correcting my grammar and the occasional blog inaccuracy. ("**Slicker** than snot on a doornail. **Not** slipperier." Duly noted.) I grew up to be an editor in spite of this.

Thank you to my son Robert. You've turned out great. Apparently years of single parenting did not screw you up too badly.

And most of all, thanks to my husband Paul. All the credit goes to you. This Chump Lady enterprise is **entirely your fault**. You told me to write a book. And when I said no, you persisted. So I said maybe a blog. That seemed more doable. And then a blog turned into a book. Every day you supported us, and worked hard, and let me write. You're an indefatigable cheerleader and the best husband ever. (I should know, I had a couple of losers before you.) I thank God every day for the idiocy of our cheating exes and the good fortune that brought you to New Orleans so I could fall in love with you. I'm blessed beyond measure to be your wife. Thank you, and you win—here's your book.

Contents

Acknowledgments	*vii*
Preface	*xi*
1. An Introduction and an Apology	1
2. Triage for the Recently Chumped	7
Start with yourself.	9
Your cheater is not your friend.	10
Do not confront until you have evidence.	11
See a lawyer.	12
Put your finances in order.	14
Find a shrink.	15
Find support.	18
Do not feel sympathy for your cheater.	20
Do not keep your cheater's secrets.	22
Do not plead for your marriage or give them "time to decide."	24
Do not discuss your feelings with them now.	24
3. Cheaters – The Way They Do The Things They Do	27
Ego Kibbles	28
The Unified Theory of Cake	30
The Humiliating Dance of "Pick Me!"	32
4. Stupid Shit Cheaters Say – And How to Respond	35
I love you but I'm not in love with you.	36
I didn't intend to hurt you.	37
You weren't meeting my needs.	38
I need time to decide.	40
We could have an open marriage. Monogamy isn't natural.	41
I don't understand your hostility.	42

But I loved you all along.	43
If you met him/her—you'd really them! He/she's a lot like you!	45
I would try to reconcile, but you're never going to forgive me.	46
I need to mourn the end of the affair.	47

5. Reconciliation – Am I a Unicorn?   49

    Real remorse and genuine imitation Naugahyde remorse   56

6. Chumps, Why Are You Stuck?   61

Untangling the Skein of Fuckupedness	62
Spackle	66
Hopium	68
Chump Fears	69
Trust That They Suck	79

7. The Fine Art of No Contact   81

Why Go No Contact?	82
Do Not Feed the Beast	83
How to Go No Contact When You Do Not Have Kids Together	85
How to Go No Contact When You Have Kids Together	86
How to Go No Contact with a Scary Wing Nut	88
The Beauty of No Contact	89

8. What Was Real? Does It Matter?   91

9. Getting to Meh   97

Fuck meh. I want revenge.	98
I'll never trust again.	101
So get over it.	107

About the Author   *111*

Preface

Before we get into the meaty business of discussing chumps and cheaters, I wanted to take a moment to explain my language. That's the beautiful thing about the prefaces to books, they're full of these little caveats and disclaimers most folks pass over. Prefaces must be the literary equivalent of "How to operate your safety belt" demonstrations on airplanes.

I have a potty mouth. I thought you should know. If you don't read the blog, you're probably unfamiliar with the intensity with which I drop eff bombs. It's not that I'm a particularly coarse person in real life. (I'm actually a WASP-y preacher's kid from the Midwest, three defects in favor of civility.) It's that I learned early on that I am incapable of writing about infidelity without cursing.

My writing is a verbal bitchslap to chumps—"Wake UP! Stop being a chump!" It's also a manifesto directed toward cheaters—a Declaration of Independence from mindfuckery. I don't regard infidelity in soft terms. You won't see the words "wayward" or "betrayed spouse" here. I see infidelity as a deliberate set of choices used to gain advantage over the unsuspecting. My language reflects that. I say "cheater" and "chump." Chump means you were more than betrayed—you were conned. Played for a fool.

Euphemisms like "wayward" muddy the intent of cheaters. Poor Wayward. He's lost. Stuck in a snow bank and can't find his way home. Won't someone come pin his address on his sweater and show him the way? Unlike Cheater, who you wouldn't pick up on the side of road lest he rob you and leave you for dead. Wayward is a poor sausage you should feel sorry for. Cheater is a guy you cross the street to avoid.

Similarly, I don't like the soppiness of "betrayed spouses." You're more than the experience of being betrayed. You got played. You're a chump. It's not a permanent condition.

As for my potty mouth, if my language offends you, consider the subject matter. What's worse? Saying "fucktard" or having to paternity test your children? "Mindfuckery" or finding your husband has been rating escorts? "Piece of shit" or explaining infidelity to your nine-year old?

But it's so… angry. Well, yes I am angry about infidelity. It's an injustice. I'm pissed off for you. You should be pissed off too. Not forever, but just long enough to motor yourself away from that clusterfuck. Anger is also the source of a lot of humor. The pomposity of cheaters is such a rich source of satire. We make them out to be so all-powerful because they've crushed our worlds. But take a step back and see how pathetic it all is. How banal cheaters are compared with the grandiose creatures they imagine themselves to be.

All to say, hey, I swear in this book, I'm sarcastic, and I draw snarky cartoons. There is a freedom in not being a mental health professional writing for a peer-reviewed journal. I'm simply an observer and I lived it. I'm a journalist and cartoonist. This isn't an academic book. I'm a fellow chump.

Another word on language—this may drive grammarians nuts but my antecedents don't match. Instead of cheater singular, then "him or her" (very awkward), I write cheater, then "them." I go from the singular to the plural. Why? Because the construct "him or her" is clunky; and I don't want to write about cheaters using gender pronouns if I can avoid it. Straight, gay, transgender, men, women all cheat. No one has the market cornered on douchebaggery. Please forgive my grammatically incorrect shortcut.

Well, that's all the words I have on words for now. Thank you for reading. Please store your suitcase in the overhead compartment…

Chapter 1

An Introduction and an Apology

I'm sorry if you need this book. If you're perusing the infidelity literature, I'll assume your interest isn't purely academic—you're a chump. You were played for a fool, lied to, and left as carrion for the divorce lawyers.

Welcome to Chump Nation. You're not alone. I'm here to tell you the pain is finite and you will get to the other side. Many chumps have walked this path before you and I'm one of them. Chump Lady is the collective wisdom I wish somebody had given me the day I woke up to find another woman's thong in my bed, that day of sickening discovery when I realized my spouse was a stranger and my marriage was a Kafka short story.

I did like a lot of chumps. I stumbled on to infidelity boards. I ordered books. I got therapy. I got conflicting messages. Reconcile! Don't reconcile! I got "remorse" from my cheater. And I got more discovery days (D-Days) of continued cheating.

What I didn't get was a decoder ring. I had no idea how to navigate that nightmare. Mostly, I struggled to understand my cheater, how to parse the self-serving nonsense that came out of his mouth. I clung to his apologies when his actions demonstrated that he wasn't terribly sorry. I projected that he must feel ashamed and lost when I had no real evidence of that. (If he's so ashamed, why does he keep doing the same damn thing over and over?) I resisted believing that I could be so terribly mistaken about this person. I wasn't a chump—oh no, I was a brave woman loving a misunderstood, broken man and we shared a love that would see us through this crisis!

By the fourth D-Day, I left. Over the span of a year and a half, between D-Days one and four, I did every stupid, chumpy, grief-stricken thing a person could do. (Consider this guide the trial-tested results of "what not to do," flubbed by yours truly.) But I did finally divorce the idiot with the loving support of my friends and family, and a virtual online world of fellow chumps.

After years spent on infidelity boards, I noticed a curious thing—other chumps were doing exactly the same stupid, chumpy, grief-stricken things that I was doing. And I noticed multitudes of cheaters behaving in uncannily similar ways to my cheater. Using the same sorry excuses. Manipulating with the same sociopathic panache. Blameshifting their shitty decisions on to chumps and feeling very, very sorry for themselves.

And it occurred to me that cheaters must work from some playbook. They were not "wayward" or lost. No, they were utterly conscious of their manipulations. But chumps kept mistakenly assuming that the cheaters were on the same team. It was as if chumps thought they were playing by the Queensbury rules, when instead they'd been suckered into a baffling match of Cheater Ball. Why are the agreed-upon rules constantly changing in absurd, unilateral directions?

"Ten point penalty for widget squiffling! I win! You're off sides! I get to kick the wombat now and you owe me seven orphans!"

"But the game isn't played with wombats."

"Oh really?" says the cheater, running for the goal post. "Catch me if you can!"

What's the point of this goofy metaphor? The entire purpose of Cheater Ball is chaos. You thought you entered marriage with an agreed upon set of rules, but your cheater was playing Cheater Ball. The goal is to keep you off balance with diversions and vagaries, so they can pursue their own agenda. The rules change at whim to benefit the cheater. Duping chumps is sport and cheaters are not sharing their playbook for a reason—they're not on the same team. Keeping you in the dark lets them "win" and keeps you at a disadvantage.

I started my blog Chump Lady in 2012 to give chumps their own playbook and explain the manipulations of cheaters. The motto at Chump Lady is "Leave a cheater, gain a life." By the time I began my blog, I'd been divorced several years and happily remarried to a fellow chump. When I was deep in the nightmare of my former marriage, I noticed another peculiar thing about the infidelity experience—the majority of infidelity resources were pro-reconciliation, especially on the Internet. It seemed there was an entire cottage industry peddling false hope about "affair proofing" one's marriage.

There was absolutely no place that was saying "leave the motherfucker, you'll feel a lot better for it." And no one was pointing out an obvious, sad truth—**you cannot save marriages by yourself.** We don't control other people. We only control ourselves. We cannot "nice" people out of affairs by being better spouses. All the loving patience in the world will not prevent someone from driving their life into a ditch if they're so inclined. And it's crazy optimistic to think that a cheater, especially a serial cheater, will undergo a character transplant. Most of them seem to prefer Cheater Ball to fair sportsmanship. Who were these mythical people who truly felt their marriage was stronger thanks to infidelity? The boards I read were full of sad, twitchy people lamenting the lack of trust in their marriages. Reconciliation seemed overhyped, over sold, and exceedingly rare.

Where were the stories of people who left cheaters and found happier lives? Where were the cheerleaders for self-respect? So much of the literature and online commentary seemed geared toward avoiding the dreaded specter of divorce. Don't be one of those pathetic divorced people! Avoid the shame of single parenthood! Screw this up and your children will be doomed! You will fail them by not keeping your marriage together, so just *try harder*. As if it wasn't bad enough to be cheated on, the very resources purported to "help" you, wanted to guilt you into owning your part of it all.

I wanted to know, why was this *my* failure? Obviously I value marriage more than my cheater, because duh, I didn't cheat. Why the divorce shame? Why isn't cheating on your spouse more shameful than divorce? Why the assumption that I could control these outcomes? What if you're left? Does that make you a failure? Or what if you file because your cheater won't pull the plug and be the bad guy? Is sticking around for the children and modeling dysfunction (abuse me and I'll just try harder to keep you) really better than leaving? Why must I "win" a cheater back, assuming that's even possible?

It just seemed to me that there was a gaping hole in the infidelity literature. Nothing I read spoke to my experience—that leaving a cheater was the sanest, healthiest thing I ever did. My world got brighter and better the minute I laid that burden down.

I'm not saying it was easy—it was scary as hell, and I screwed up a number of times trying to get there, but in the end I did it—I left him. My chump credentials are pretty slim compared to people who've had long marriages and children with serial cheaters. My husband, a fellow chump, had a marriage of over two decades and two children with a serial cheater. I understand the sunk costs. Mercifully, I served a lighter sentence.

When I discovered my ex was cheating, I had only been married six months. His mistress called me to inform me of her existence. (I had found her thong in bed a couple weeks earlier; we were both snooping to discover the other.) Turns out, he had a double life spanning back at least 20 years. I had just moved away from my home of 16 years to a no-fault divorce state. I'd given up my job, moved my son, and bought a house with him (with my cash down payment and his credit). I was utterly screwed. It took nearly two years to extract myself from that mess, to find a job, to get a settlement, to accept what I had lost. I had to reinvent my entire life all over again.

So when I say "Leave a cheater, gain a life"—I'm speaking from experience. I'm not being flippant about divorce or starting over—it's incredibly challenging. But being married to a remorseless cheater is a million times more difficult. **It's slow soul death.**

When I was slogging through infidelity, I wish I had the knowledge of my future self—that I would remarry a wonderful man who cherishes and respects me. That marriage could be so much better than a playing a bit part in some narcissist's soap opera. That my son would turn out fine, and heave a sigh of relief to be out of the drama. That all that energy I was throwing at a cheater was now mine to invest in myself. And I did exactly that—I was more peaceful, more creative, I took on more writing assignments, I learned to weld, I gardened, I was a happier parent and a better friend.

So why weren't other successful survivors of infidelity telling their stories? Heck, I knew a bunch of them. My neighbor once left her wealthy cheater husband, was a single mother to four kids, raised them in a rough part of town, while putting herself through nursing school. The kids are now grown, and she's been happily remarried for 30 years to an academic who never had kids of his own and embraced her family. The cheater married his affair partner, descended into alcoholism and lost his money.

Or my friend's brother who nearly burned to death in a military explosion. His wife took that opportunity, while he was in intensive care, to tell him she was leaving him for his best friend and taking their infant son with her. Yeah, *that* guy survived. He eventually remarried a lovely woman his sister fixed him up with and they've been together over 20 years and raised two kids.

Or my aunt, who left an alcoholic, cheating lawyer in Chicago. Took her years to get a divorce. It was the 1970s and women couldn't get loans back then without their husbands' signatures. She couldn't afford a divorce lawyer, until her boss co-signed a loan to pay for her retainer. She raised two kids on her own, until eventually marrying her high school sweetheart, a fellow chump, whose wife ran off with the town priest. They've been together nearly 30 years. Her ex died years ago of alcoholism.

Why don't people like that publicize their stories? Because, in my opinion, few people who survive infidelity want to relive the experience, let alone shepherd a new crop of chumps to the other side. They're busy living their saner lives, why revisit the nightmare? They know it's a nightmare, and generally you'll know these former chumps by their compassion. They'll tell you their story after you've gone through yours.

Once I started my blog, I began to collect other people's success stories. Clearly, not everyone's happy ending is a remarriage. (The folks I know, it's several decades since their D-Days. I do think, however, that chumps make good partners and tend to couple up again successfully later.) Thousands of people have written to me to say they went back to school, bought their own homes, reared good kids, got ahead in their careers, found their passion again. And yep, many of them remarry fellow chumps. Many of the stories are impossibly heroic—she passed the bar exam during a D-Day; she found out while 6 months pregnant and filed for divorce; he got custody of the kids after she abandoned them. I file these stories under "You Are Mighty." No one writes to say, years out, I regretted my decision leaving a cheater. I hear time and again—I wish I had done this sooner. I can't believe I lived this way for so long. As my aunt put it after her ex moved out: "The walls in your house sing again."

Revisiting the nightmare of infidelity seemed to be the stand alone job of the reconciliation industry—people haunted by this shit years after the fact, "standing" for their marriage, trying desperately to save marriages by themselves, and "triggering" still.

By the time people find me, they've often tried all that. I created Chump Lady to be a place that was not focused on saving marriages—but rather a haven for chumps to save their sanity.

I wrote this book to be the toolkit I wish I'd had, the decoder ring no one gave me. Chump Lady translates the manipulations of infidelity and gives you a language to understand this baffling, painful experience. So here's your step-by-step guide to navigating your way out of this shit storm—full of advice, gallows humor, and cartoons deflating the pomposity of cheaters.

You can do this. Chump Nation has got your back.

Chapter 2

Triage for the Recently Chumped

This chapter is for those of you who just found out and may still be curled in the fetal position. It's time to take back your power. Pause for a moment from the vomiting and crying and find your badass.

I know you're in shock, and I know you're grieving, but let's be a field marshal now and not a damp mess spilled over the furniture. So many chumps react to infidelity with paralysis, afraid that any misstep will drive their cheater even further away from them. Wrong impulse. Your cheater is already out in the wild blue yonder of the affair. Denial, appeasement, or trying to "nice" someone out of an affair are tactics doomed to failure. What you need to do right now is **draw some firm boundaries and enforce them**.

But before I get into the particulars, let me skip to the end of the story and tell you how it ends—**you survive this**. Actually, you're going to be triumphant. Yes, it's going to hurt like a motherfucker, yes, it's going to test your mettle, and you'll probably screw up a few times—but you *will* overcome.

How do I know? Because **what's the alternative**? Let this shit define you? Get pulled into the undertow and drown? Become one of those brittle cyborg people fronting a fake life, writing insipid holiday newsletters that never reveal what a sham they've become? Is that what you want? To lose your soul?

Look, cheaters might try and take your kids, your house, your retirement accounts, your wedding china, and your dignity, but they cannot have your fucking **soul**. You own that. Infidelity will **not** break you. It's a sucker punch to the gut, but it's not a death sentence. It's a horrible loss. A loss of trust, of innocence, of personal safety, of family as you thought you knew it. There's so much to grieve and I won't lie to you, processing all feels like it will take forever. You can't hurry the misery along, you just feel it, but I promise it's **finite**.

If you let this pain crack open your heart, and you accept the vulnerability and chaos, you're going to be a better person for it. **You will never be smug again**. And that right there makes you 99 percent less of an asshole than most of the general population. You're a survivor who knows what every other disaster survivor knows—life can be unjust, random, and cruel. You cannot question the wreckage, you can only rebuild. And the only people who are worth spit are the people who aren't afraid of your pain, who'll walk into your cracked open heart and not blame you for it.

DON'T ASK THIS GUY'S OPINION

"What did you do to make this bad thing happen to you?" **Fuck those people**. You were chumped. Someone's crappy, entitled behavior did this to you. You trusted and got played. You don't control what happens to you, but you do get to control how you're going to respond. Begin by having some compassion for yourself. Be a better person for this lousy hand you were dealt. You've now got the ability to walk into other people's cracked open hearts because you **get it** and while that might not feel like a gift right now, it is a huge gift. You will appreciate every good thing that comes after this and every good person. You will see the world in Technicolor. You'll know who your friends are and who is a waste of space. You'll be wiser and stronger. A farmer I know calls these sorts of gifts "hard blessings." Not obvious blessings, but the kind that come after a devastating hailstorm wipes out your crops.

Infidelity is no measure of your worth or of your lovability. One idiot betrayed you. That's one idiot's opinion of your worth and consider the source—a cheater. You don't share the same values. Would you ask your local tinfoil-hat-wearing schizophrenic to weigh in on your lovability? Of course not, because you don't see the world in the same way as a crazy person. Your cheater hears voices from outer space too, but it's more of a droning "me, me, me" sound.

Anyway, my point is—buck up. You can work on your grieving and what it all means later, the important thing right now is to **protect yourself**.

Start with yourself.

Let me get the mom stuff out the way first. Are you eating? Are you sleeping?

Getting through infidelity is a marathon and you need to fuel accordingly. You may skip over this advice thinking it banal, but it isn't. The shock of betrayal takes an incredible toll on your body. It's a monumental amount of stress. You need to keep your wits about you and that's absolutely impossible with insomnia or an empty stomach.

If you can't eat, try those protein shakes, soup, anything fortifying and liquid. If you can't sleep—see your doctor immediately and get some Ambien. In fact, before you consider antidepressants, consider a temporary sleep aid. Your mind may be crazed because of sleep depravation.

Exercise. Whether that's walking the dog, or hitting the gym—nothing makes you feel more in control of yourself and manages your stress like exercising. It will help with the sleep too.

You've just been ambushed and you need to prepare for the battle ahead. Take care of yourself emotionally and physically. The longer you stay in a state of disbelief and paralysis, the more opportunity your cheater has to keep taking advantage of you.

Which brings me to my first guiding principle:

Your cheater is not your friend.

Remember what I said about cheaters not playing by the same set of rules as you? You just woke up to find out you're in the fifth inning of Cheater Ball. When did the game start? What's the score? Your cheater isn't going to tell you. For cheaters, part of the game of Cheater Ball is denying they're playing Cheater Ball. Work from the assumption that your cheater has a very different agenda than you do and that your well-being is not at the top of it.

YOU'RE SO INDEPENDENT. I DIDN'T THINK YOU NEEDED ALL OF ME.

Cheaters' actions clearly demonstrate that it is all about them. Affairs are decided upon **unilaterally**. Your cheater did not consider your health, your feelings, your children, or your shared finances. So why would you think you can achieve consensus with this person now? **There is no great awakening**. Discovery does not transform cheaters into honorable people. It does not make them suddenly appreciate what they could lose. No, discovery kicks their manipulation game up several notches. Cheaters want very desperately for you to go right back to being their malleable, chump-in-the-dark and to prevent ugly consequences from raining down upon them. The best way to make sure that happens is manipulation.

Actually, manipulation is just a continuation of their existing strategy. They've been manipulating you all along. You can't cheat on someone without lying to or gaslighting them. They're not about to change tactics and lead with unvarnished honesty now. **Remain highly skeptical.** Judge your cheater by their actions over time—a *long* time. Don't assume friendship and mutuality where it doesn't exist. Your job right now is to protect yourself and your children from further harm. That doesn't make you churlish, selfish, or unkind (things your cheater may accuse you of). That makes you a smart person who is enforcing his or her boundaries.

How do you protect yourself?

Do not confront until you have evidence.

Most cheaters will lie and gaslight you unless you catch them dead to rights, and even then they usually only cop to what they think you already know. If you confront them before you have evidence, there's a good chance they'll take the affair further underground.

If you've discovered evidence of an affair, or someone has outed an affair to you, put all your evidence in a safe place (preferably a lawyer's office in a fault divorce state) before you confront your cheater. Email it to a trusted friend, to another account you've set up, put it in a safety deposit box. Never reveal your sources.

If you're in the fortunate position of knowing you're a chump before your cheater knows you know—you've got a tactical advantage. You can line up your financial and legal ducks in a row without interference.

If your discovery was sloppier (as it often is), if the cheater confessed, if you stumbled across evidence of an affair in front of your spouse, or if you lost your shit before you read this—don't worry. You can still put your affairs in order (I pun). It's just going to be more difficult because your cheater will be pulling out the stops to keep you from imposing consequences. Just stay strong and keep protecting yourself.

See a lawyer.

But! But! This is all a terrible misunderstanding and they're very sorry and you're going to work it out! Okay. Please, still see a lawyer.

Why? Because you're a chump. You've demonstrated you can be played. Your cheater is counting on that and now that the infidelity has been discovered, don't rely on them to do right by you. No, the pressure is on to manipulate you further. You need the cool head of legal advocacy. Even if you do not divorce, seeing a lawyer means you know exactly what your rights are, what you could be entitled to in a divorce, what decisions you should and should not make concerning your finances, your children, exposure of the affair, moving out, having sex with your spouse after discovery, abandonment, temporary support, etc.

Another reason to see a lawyer is that your cheater may have already done so. Don't assume it will always be you who will have the option of pulling the plug. Your cheater already has one foot out the door in this marriage; they could abandon you at any time.

I know seeing a lawyer makes it real and scary, especially if you're not ready for the "D" word yet. It can feel like putting the cart before the horse. *I haven't decided yet if reconciliation is possible! Won't I antagonize my spouse by seeing a lawyer?*

First of all, don't worry about antagonizing your cheater. Seeking legal counsel is not a sin analogous with infidelity. Your cheater certainly didn't worry about antagonizing you with an affair. Just see a lawyer, don't announce it to your cheater. Just do it.

Second of all, you are in **crisis**. Bitchslap yourself, please. You need professional help to sort through this mess, and your lawyer has seen it all before and knows how to navigate this. Admit it—you do not possess this skill set.

People who will cheat on you may be fucking you over a multitude of other ways as well—especially financially. Never say to yourself "Oh they would never…" **Yes they would**. In my experience of cheaters, nothing is terribly sacred—your bed, your pension, your children's college funds. Let's hope the entitlement doesn't run that deep, but don't bank on it. That's why you need legal advice. Lawyers know what moves cheaters may make and how to block those moves, or mitigate the damage legally. Knowledge is power. The very **worst** thing you can do is trust the cheater who created this clusterfuck to set things right. No, **go on the offensive.** You find out what is in your best legal interest and you call the tune on any potential reconciliation. If you aren't hiring this lawyer for your divorce, you're damn sure hiring them to draw up your post-nup.

What's a post-nup? Talk to a lawyer, it can vary state-to-state, but it is an uncontested divorce settlement. Like a pre-nup, a post-nup is a ready-made settlement in case of divorce, which sets out the terms of asset division and custody if appropriate. If you reconcile, you're taking a risk that your cheater will not cheat again. A post-nup is your "get out of jail free" card if they do cheat again or you just can't hack reconciliation.

Remember—**sorry is as sorry does**. Only cheaters control whether or not they cheat again, so a remorseful cheater should be keen to sign a post-nup—because it's a useless document, right? Because they're not going to cheat again, right? Because they want to demonstrate their remorse, right?

You cannot put provisions in a post-nup like "If you cheat again I get to gouge your eyes out with a rusty spoon." It's simply an uncontested divorce settlement. (For more on calculating your odds of successful reconciliation see Chapter 5, Reconciliation – Am I a Unicorn?)

How do you find a lawyer? Asking for a referral can be awkward. If you ask someone you know, you've let the cat out of the bag that yes, you're having marital difficulties. You might not be ready for that. So consider the anonymity of an online community or referral service. SuperLawyers.com is good resource. (No, they don't pay me to plug them, I just happen to be married to a Super Lawyer.) Super Lawyers are the lawyers who other lawyers recommend; they're the top tier in their field.

Make sure you get a **family law lawyer**. Do **not** get a general practice lawyer. Do not hire your friend's brother-in-law who will do it as a favor, fitting it in when he can. Do **not** try to do this yourself with the help of a youtube video, a self-help article, and a couple shots of tequila. Hire a professional—a family law professional. You wouldn't hire a podiatrist for your sinus surgery—don't hire the wrong kind of lawyer.

How do you afford a lawyer? You bite the bullet. Getting the right sort of settlement will anticipate various scenarios and can save you a lot of money in the long run. For many lawyers, the first hour of consolation is free, so consult with a few and see who feels like a good fit. Ask about their payment terms and retainer fees. Don't cheap out on this—take a loan from your family if you must, pawn jewelry, run up your credit card—but do get proper legal advice. If you're truly broke or financially dependent on your cheater, call your local Legal Aid society. Help is out there.

And remember—lawyers bill in six-minute increments. **Your lawyer is not your therapist**. Just stick to business.

Put your finances in order.

Make copies all your financial documents, retirement accounts, and credit reports. Know how much debt you have. If your cheater wants to reconcile, demand a recent credit report from them. This will reveal hidden credit cards, debts, and P.O. boxes they may have used to conduct the affair. If they balk —there's your answer. There's shit in there they don't want you to know about.

If you own a business with your cheater, if you have complicated assets, consider the services of a forensic accountant. Monies spent on an affair are marital assets and can be asked for back in a divorce. If you've got a complex financial situation, hire a professional to follow the money trail.

If you are financially dependent on your cheater, if your cheater moved out and abandoned you, if you have minor children to support—a lawyer can go to court to get immediate temporary support orders.

Unfortunately, financial abuse often goes with infidelity—so don't take it laying down. Get professional help.

Find a shrink.

When shopping for a shrink, ask them about their infidelity experience. Sometimes you have to try out a few people before you find someone you're comfortable with. Avoid bearded men in sweater vests. Okay, *not really*. That's just a tiny prejudice I have, but anyone who mutters banalities like "you need to dialogue" or listens to a litany of abuse and weakly inquires, "and how does that make you *feel?*" is a nitwit.

Look, I have a lot of respect for the mental health profession, but there are infidelity quacks out there. What makes a quack? Anyone who offers to "affair proof" your marriage, or has some cult-like program that promises marital success regardless of what your cheater does. You're vulnerable; please avoid the charlatans.

More mainstream quackery buys into the nonsense that you can control other people through your behavior. That you can "nice" someone back into a marriage and that your "unkindness" drove them to cheat in the first place. Anyone who wants you to accept your part of another's cheating is, in my opinion, a quack. We don't ask victims of domestic abuse to accept their part in another's slamming them headfirst through a plate glass window, and we don't ask partners of alcoholics to discuss what they did to drive this person to drink. So do not accept a therapist who asks you what you did to "contribute" to the affair. The answer to that question is—"I trusted them."

Infidelity quacks operate from several flawed assumptions:

1. That people cheat because of something lacking in the other spouse.
2. That infidelity is just a symptom of larger marital issues and is not the main event worth discussing.
3. That you can "nice" people out of cheating.

Let's take the quackery point by point.

1. People cheat because something is lacking in *them* — connection, empathy, good character. Cheating is about entitlement, narcissism, and opportunity. You might actually be a crappy spouse, but you did not make your spouse cheat. That decision is on them 100 percent. There was a giant decision tree of available options—cheating was the rotten branch they chose.

2. Once someone decides to cheat—*that* is the bullet in the marriage. Infidelity is the issue that needs addressing first before you get into your love languages, communication styles, and your family history. There is no point in discussing any of the rest of your marital relationship when one party is actively not committed to the marriage. It's like choosing dinner selections on the Hindenburg.

3. Cheaters don't need insight that cheating is wrong. They don't need a shrink feeding their already inflated appetite for attention, asking them about themselves and their childhood hang-ups. Cheaters *know* what the rules are—they just don't think the rules should apply to them. They need to be called out on that shit—or as shrinks put it, their "disordered thoughts." This isn't about how nice *you* are or are not, it's about how entitled *they* are.[1]

Now back to you. You may do marriage counseling, you may not, but do get your own shrink to help you through this. A good shrink will

---

1. For more reading about the proper approach to therapy with disturbed characters check out Dr. George Simon's blog www.manipulative-people.com. He has a lot to say about traditional therapy and how it doesn't take into account character or personality disorders.

challenge you, but only about what you actually control—yourself. A good shrink will tell you to listen to yourself, figure out your boundaries, and give you strategies to enforce them. A good shrink will probably spend some time examining your chumpiness.

There is a difference between self-examination and self-recrimination. The problem with chumps is that we are usually already terrifically accomplished at blaming ourselves (and cheaters are great at blaming us too). We don't need any help in that quarter, so a shrink who encourages that "I drove them to it" mentality can inflict further harm. *Oh, I'm the problem, you say? I'll just spend several years here stuck trying to cure myself in order to fix this person who is abusing me!* Chumps like the idea that they could control this outcome. But self-examination asks instead: "What am I doing here? What are my values? Is this an acceptable relationship to me?"

When I went through infidelity, I saw several therapists. Most of them were good; one of them was bearded, sweater vested, and dreadful (inspiring the cartoon); and one was truly excellent—Janet. She was a tiny, fiery woman with a potty mouth who wasn't afraid to call my cheater on his shit, or me on mine.

My cheater said patently stupid things in therapy such as: "I like being a narcissist" or he would refer to his affairs as a mistake (singular), like forgetting to buy milk. Janet would shout at me: "ARE YOU LISTENING TO THIS? THIS IS WHO HE IS!" It wasn't a joke. It was his character. He was revealing himself. He had been all along, but I was being such a hopeful idiot I wasn't paying close enough attention.

She told me I was "exquisitely co-dependent." Ouch. That stung. Me? I am a strong, independent person in a difficult marriage! Co-dependent? I had to chew on that.

But she was right. I was focusing way too much on my cheater and what made him tick and what he would do next more than I was on myself. She called me to the carpet on my chumpiness.

As for my cheater? She told him that he had his "head stuck up his ass," that he was greedy, that he needed to learn what love was. She didn't pull any punches.

When my ex would try and give her a line about how he "didn't remember" where he was on Christmas Day or with whom, she yelled at him "BULLSHIT! I'M A JEW. EVEN *I* KNOW WHAT I WAS DOING ON CHRISTMAS!"

God love her, she wasn't nice—she was effective. The best advice I can give you on finding a therapist is look for a tiny, Jewish woman who swears like a sailor. Choose a Janet. Avoid the meek and sweater vested.

Find support.

It's totally normal to be emotionally sloppy in the beginning. Some poor acquaintance asks how you are—and you will inevitably over share. "Sharon left me for a Dobro player she met on Facebook. Some weasel-faced douchebag with a soul patch. Been fucking him for months before I found out. She used to hate facial hair and country music, but *no*, they're *soul mates*. Try explaining divorce to a 6 year old…"

The weight of fresh infidelity is like balancing an invisible bucket of toxic slop on your head all day. You try and step carefully, but sometimes you lose balance and… splat. It spills all over everything.

You need a safe place to spill. Not everyone gets it. A therapist's office is good, but if you're like most chumps, you'll look for an online support group and want to compare notes with compassionate strangers 24/7. How chumps survived before Google, I have no idea.

There is great comfort in finding fellow chumps who are living this nightmare in real time with you. For one thing, you'll discover this crap is very common. You aren't freak of the week. You'll notice your cheater is doing and saying almost the identical things to cheaters everywhere. You'll find people slightly ahead of you on this journey who can offer comfort, and people slightly behind you who *you* can comfort.

I encourage you to find some chump solidarity if for no other reason than the people nearest to you tend not to understand the trauma of infidelity if they haven't lived it. They can get compassion fatigue if you lean on them too much and in frustration may tell you to "get over it." An online community can be your safety valve. You can vent to them and spill your bucket of toxic slop where they've spilled theirs. Let the people in your real life help you with logistics, watch your kids for a few hours, bring you dinner, distract you with their company. Find a safe place for your pain.

Unfortunately, not everyone is a safe place. Infidelity is a good opportunity to sort the wheat from the chaff. The good ones will rally around you and even if they haven't lived it, they will respond with compassion. You may find support from folks you didn't know that well until this happened. The dross will avoid you like you're contagious. Some people will feel threatened by your vulnerability and comfort themselves with the notion that you did something wrong to make this happen to you—meaning they're safe. It couldn't possibly happen to them.

Others people will plead neutrality, which is about them. They don't want to have to think of your cheater differently, they would prefer everyone go back to happier, ignorant times. They don't want to contend with the awkwardness, so please eat the shit sandwich for their sake. People like this aren't your friends. You don't share the same values. If someone can't feel appalled at your spouse betraying you, if that only engenders feelings of "neutrality"? I think you can find a better class of friend.

When it comes to finding online support, of course, I will plug my own forum www.chumplady.com—but there are other good ones out there as well.

My only word of caution is steer clear of the reconciliation charlatans. There are many places that prey on vulnerable chumps. If the site owners have big shiny hair and sell motivational DVDs on affair proofing—keep googling. Affair proofing is the infidelity scam equivalent of car undercoating and paint protection. You don't need those services. You need the solidarity of fellow chumps.

Do not feel sympathy for your cheater.

I know you probably still love this person, and that's tragic, but right now you need to love yourself more. Reserve your compassion for yourself, not the sad sausage who just fucked their way into this mess.

Cheaters often display emotion when their affairs are discovered, but if you pay attention, it's usually sympathy for themselves—not the pain they inflicted on you. What consequences are you going to impose on them? Whatever will people think? How will they live without their affair partner? Who did you tell? What do you know? Can't you see how *very difficult* on this is on them? Your pain is very upsetting.

Your pain is upsetting not in the empathetic sense of "it hurts me to see you hurt," but in the "shut the fuck up already" sense.

I tend to divide cheaters into two camps. Those who attempt remorse and those who step over your crumpled, sobbing body and go fix themselves a Hot Pocket. The Hot Pocket cheaters usually sleep like babies too, totally untroubled by their betrayals. In my opinion, the Hot Pocket cheaters are sociopaths. No adaptive anxiety, they're totally chill and indifferent to your agony.

The remorse cheaters probably care, just not as much as they should and certainly not as much as they care about themselves. What would be splendid is if you could just return to unknowing chumpdom and stop putting a cramp on their lifestyle.

If you resist? They know the way to your heartstrings. You care about them. So they play the self-pity card. You've always made their needs central before—why stop now?

Nothing underscores cheaters' entitlement more than wanting sympathy from the very person they just gutted.

Disordered people (and we can argue later about whether cheaters are permanently disordered or it's situational) have three channels when it comes to manipulation after discovery—charm, rage, and self-pity.

Charm

"I'll do anything to make this up to you." "It didn't mean anything." And the whole mess makes them horny.

You're being seduced by a con. Talk to a lawyer before you engage in any post-affair sex (otherwise known as "hysterical bonding.") Some fault states construe this as forgiveness. And don't think your cheater doesn't know that.

Rage

Screaming at you. Making threats. Blaming you for the cheating. Infidelity is abuse, and now they're just overtly ramping it up.

If a cheater threatens your life, get a protection from abuse order. They do not have to hit you for it to be considered abuse. The law also takes verbal threats seriously.

And whatever you do, do not react to their provocations. If you can keep a voice recorder on you, do it. (It's not legal in all states). The real crazies will look for an excuse to charge *you* with abuse—do not give them one.

Self-Pity

Throwing you off the scent of their misdeeds by distracting you with *their* pain.

Some go so far as to threaten suicide. If your cheater threatens self-harm, **always** take this seriously. Call the authorities immediately and have them committed for an involuntary psych evaluation.

If they meant it, they will get the help they need. If they said it to manipulate you, they'll never try that shit again.

In summary, have boundaries with your cheater. Now is the time to focus on *your* healing. You don't have the wherewithal to carry the cheater's burdens as well, however much you might still love them.

Do not keep your cheater's secrets.

Infidelity is not your shame to wear. Speak your truth—you were cheated on. Tell whomever you want to tell.

Cheaters often want to have it both ways on disclosure. On the one hand, it's no big deal. Everyone makes "mistakes" and they don't understand why you are making such a big deal about this! Or the affair is the Great Love of their life, and it's just bigger than you both… **but don't tell anyone about it.** Huh? Don't tell anyone about the inconsequential happenstance that didn't mean anything? Or don't tell anyone about the Compelling Life Event that is the most wonderful love of the ages? *What?*

Generally what this means is—don't stray from the cheater's narrative. Don't get out there in front with your ugly "bitterness."

Look, you're not a public relations outfit. They fired you from the image polishing job when they cheated on you.

If you find yourself disclosing infidelity, my advice to you is keep it classy, truthful, and refrain from editorializing (except to your closest friends). Some favored disclosing statements are "I got divorced because I didn't like his girlfriend." "I believe a marriage is just between two people." Or simply, "She cheated on me."

You don't want to go out there and emotionally vomit all over everyone's shoes. Although a certain amount of that is often pretty unavoidable in the early days.

"Would you like fries with that?"

"My husband has been hooking up on Craiglist casual encounters! (sob)"

If it makes you feel any better, when I had my first D-Day, I had to write an $8,000 check (out of my personal account, naturally, I'm a chump...) to the guy installing our new furnace. I burst into tears and told him I'd just learned my husband was cheating on me. He looked at me horrified, and then in told me he was going to "hold me up to Jesus in prayer." Awkward, to say the least. But very kind.

Anyway, some emotional sloppiness is to be expected when you're in shock. Forgive yourself. Reserve your fortitude for the real bomb drops—family, close friends, and children.

Many people get hung up on whether they should disclose the affair to their children. My answer on that is yes, absolutely disclose. But do it age appropriately and do it without editorializing. For example, "Mommy was cheating and that's why I've been so upset." Versus, "Mommy is a whore." Children deserve the truth and gaslighting is still gaslighting, even if done with the best of intentions. *Pay no attention to daddy's catatonic state. It's just a stomach bug.*

Kids aren't stupid. They sense when something's up. Hell, unfortunately, they often know about the affair before you did and got introduced to "Daddy's friend" or "Mommy's special co-worker." If you don't tell, if you go with some euphemism that "people fall out of love," then children are stuck with this notion that love is a nebulous vapor that simply evaporates. The cloud of doom just descends on innocent families and people fall out of love! Versus the truth—life has deal breakers. And when you do Bad Things, Bad Things result.

Yes, infidelity is a painful truth for a child. But truth is a lot less scary than undefined, nameless tragedy. Children of any age understand rules and the consequences that result when rules are broken. One way to explain it to a child is: "When people get married, they promise to be each other's special person. You can't have other special boyfriends or girlfriends. Daddy broke that promise to mommy, and that's why mommy is so sad and upset."

Some people don't disclose affairs because they think (perhaps rightly) that doing so means the people in their life will hate the cheater and this will torpedo any chance they have at reconciliation. If that's the case, consider that you're protecting the cheater from the consequence of other people's bad opinion of them. And repairing their reputation is part of the painful work of honest reckoning. By not telling, you're also denying yourself the support from people who care about you.

All to say—spill it, chumps.

Do not plead for your marriage or give them "time to decide."

If your cheater is on the fence about your marriage after discovery—shut that down. Ever heard the expression—don't make anyone a priority who only makes you an option? You are not an option. You are their spouse. **This is not a contest**. They made a commitment to **you**. They don't get to renegotiate the terms. Stalling for time, acting all vague about how they intend to make this right, talking a good game and never coming through on the particulars—these are all ploys to keep them in the affair.

You **cannot** "nice" someone out of an affair. Oh, I'll just make my needs smaller and smaller, or I'll be so wonderful I'll win them back! are losing strategies. All you do with appeasement is give the cheater the green light to abuse you further.

Maintain your dignity and do not beg for your marriage. When you beg, all you do is feed their egos and give them *your* power. Now is the time to practice detachment and self care. Set aside your grief and make room for righteous anger. Let it fuel you forward. You are not a consolation prize.

It's not enough to say you're not a consolation prize, you have to live it. This is what enforcing a boundary looks like—the cheater decides to commit to the marriage then and there—or you put their crap in Hefty bags and throw it on the lawn for the raccoons.

Do not discuss your feelings with them now.

Cheaters don't give a shit. Maybe later, try an honest conversation in marriage counseling. But right now, after the affair has been discovered, your cheater can pretty much guess your emotional state—you're devastated and angry. Which to them is kind of a buzzkill… and hey, did someone say "Hot Pocket?"

Anyway, you weren't supposed to find out. And now that you know, they're losing control, and most of what you say is an annoying buzz. So let your actions do the speaking for you—you will not be accepting this abuse.

When you're dealing with narcissists (and cheating is a narcissistic act), no contact is an effective tool because it denies narcissists the essential information that they need to mindfuck you. To manipulate someone, you need to know what their buttons are. When you tell a narcissist, "Hey, this REALLY UPSETS ME"—you just handed them your button.

So be an enigma. Don't show them your vulnerable underbelly. Don't try to plead or reason with them, or tell them you care. More than just being attention and centrality to the cheater (which they love), it's **power**. I know you don't see it that way, but you're not empathy and character deficient the way they are. This person has just demonstrated to you in the most intimate and humiliating way, how little respect they have for your feelings. So it stands to reason that they cannot be trusted with **more** of your feelings.

Please just take care of yourself right now, and surround yourself with people who truly care for you. It's natural to long to be comforted and held by the very person who shattered you, to have them explain everything, and make it better, but you must resist that urge now.

Your cheater is not your friend. Everything has changed. Or really, it had already changed, but you were in the dark. Now you have a dawning awareness how badly you've been played for a chump. Take heart, chumpdom is not a permanent condition; you just need a roadmap out of this place.

The next chapter we'll begin by examining cheaters, and what makes them tick.

Chapter 3

Cheaters – The Way They Do The Things They Do

Cheating is an act of narcissism. (Of course, cheaters don't see it that way. Usually they cast it as selflessly liberating someone from the oppressive bonds of sexless marriage to a jerk.) As much as some would like to believe infidelity "just happens," cheating comes down to personal choice. Cheaters cheat because they can. Because they value their autonomy to engage in affairs more than they value your well-being. It's really that simple.

Drawing that conclusion is terribly painful of course, so chumps become deeply invested in believing it is all way more complicated than that. Surely there must be subterranean forces that motivate cheaters toward betrayal—a midlife crisis, family of origin (FOO) issues, their astrological sign, their addiction issues, their sexual confusion, their birth order, their purportedly low self esteem. (Judging by their actions, cheaters think they're quite splendid. I would argue they don't suffer from low self esteem, so much as an over abundance of self regard.)

Chumps direct a lot of energy at trying to figure cheaters out and even more energy at blaming themselves. *God, maybe it's me. I made them do this. I wasn't meeting their needs.*

Look, you might actually suck. I tend to doubt it, but let's say for the sake of argument you're truly dreadful. **You didn't make your cheater cheat.** At any point your

cheater could've had an honest conversation with you, or a therapist, or a divorce attorney. They didn't do that. They cheated.

But chances are that you don't suck. If I were to bet, I'd say you're the more invested partner—the person who brought more to the relationship and shouldered more than your share of responsibilities. Affairs take time and energy away from relationships; someone has to pick up the slack. As you weren't the person fucking around, I'd say that person was you—an imperfect person, but a committed one. You loved with your whole heart and you got chumped.

So don't buy any of this "unmet needs" nonsense. You didn't cause the cheating, and sadly, you can't control it. You only get to control yourself. So instead of focusing on your cheater's motivations, ask yourself the harder question—why am I hanging around this jerk who's not my friend?

Friends don't betray you. Whatever their protestations to the contrary, that they "loved you all along," or they "love you but aren't in love with you," know this—it's all about them. **Cheaters act out of entitlement**. Everything you need to know about the dynamics of cheating can be understood through these three concepts: **ego kibbles**, **cake**, and the **"pick me" dance**. Ego kibbles are the currency of entitlement. Cake is the situation in which the cheater has both the spouse and the affair partner. And the "pick me" dance is the dynamic by which the cheater goads the spouse and the affair partner into competing for the cheater (thereby perpetuating cake).

Master these three concepts and you'll spot the mindfuckery from a mile off.

Ego Kibbles

Cheaters need lots and lots of kibbles. Shrinks call ego kibbles "narcissistic supply," but I prefer to think in terms of Narcissist Ego Chow. Cheaters need to feed. They need lots of validation that they're special, sexy, and understood by only a special chosen few. The problem is, ego kibbles are not very sating, and so cheaters are always looking for ways to maximize kibble production.

Part of that is the cheater—they've got a hole in their soul where empathy and connection should be. So, a person can shovel ego kibbles at the cheater, but they don't fill up. They require multiple sources of kibbles to feel remotely okay, but never quite sated.

The other part of the kibble equation is the unfulfilling quality of ego kibbles themselves. Narcissistic supply is like bad chicken feed. It's cheap, commercial-grade filler. It's crap.

What's in a bag of Narcissist Ego Chow? Flattery. Attention. Easy sex. Admiration without accomplishment. Shallow attachment. Infatuation. Fantasy. Centrality.

Cheaters prefer kibbles to love. Love requires reciprocity and connection. Love is messy and demanding. Kibbles are easier.

The preference for kibbles over real love is very hard for chumps to comprehend. Chumps project the depths of their love and commitment on to cheaters, who are really just kibble-deep shallow pools. How could your cheater walk away from 20 years of marriage and three kids? Simple. They aren't that deep. They traffic in kibbles. You ascribed depth and connection to a person who doesn't possess those qualities. You don't have the same values.

When cheaters want shiny new kibbles, you've probably committed the unspeakable offense of having needs or directing your energies to someone who wasn't the cheater, like your children, for example. Maybe you got old, tired, or sick. In any case, from the cheaters' perspective, you ceased to be of use. You could not keep up with kibble demand.

Did your cheater leave but keeps coming back to you, messing with your head to see if you still

care? Kibbles! Do they want your sympathy for how hard all this is on *them*? Kibbles! Would they like to still be friends if you could just get over it and quit being a bitter killjoy? Kibbles!

See how that works? You may not be the primary source of kibbles, but you're always welcome to be an auxiliary source. You can do that by pining, engaging in drama, and keeping the cheater central in all things. Which leads us to our next nugget of cheater manipulation—cake. The best way to maximize kibble production is never giving up a kibble source.

The Unified Theory of Cake

Cake eating is the preferred Nirvanic state of the unrepentant cheater. It's the situation in which the cheater has the affair partner and the spouse. ("Having your cake and eating it too.") In fact, cake is a preferred lifestyle for many.

Ideally, the spouse is unaware of the affair partner, because that means the cheater has unfettered access to cake. After discovery, however, many cheaters will go to tremendous lengths to maintain cake. Cake eating is confusing to chumps. Chumps tend to think of affairs as competitions—it's me or him! Or what does she have that I don't have? Chumps see marriage through their own lens, of monogamy and commitment to one person. If they are not committed to me, a chump thinks, then they're for the fuckbuddy. So who's it gonna be?

Cake eaters do nothing to dissuade a distraught chump from this line of thinking. They would prefer a competition in which they are the center of the drama—all attention is on them! And a catfight ensues over their fabulousness. Cheaters would prefer you not discover their cheating, but if it must be revealed, this is how they'd like to see it play out. You try harder to win them back and maybe if you're lucky, they'll choose you!

The goal of cake is **not to choose**. Chumps often go painful round after painful round as the cheater "commits" to the marriage and then retreats. Swears to be faithful to the spouse, and then is caught again with the affair partner. Makes promises to both the chump (and the affair partner), and breaks them.

The cheater is NOT trying to decide between two people—the cheater is trying to **maintain cake**. Cake eaters are NOT confused. They are deliberately trying to maintain an unfair situation at your expense.

Cake eaters act vague. They need time. They appeal to you for patience. They feel very, very sorry for themselves. They'll assert that they're trying very hard to appease you (they're not, but they may throw you a bone like marriage counseling, or sex, or paying attention to their children), but you're so unreasonable with your demands. Cake eaters are defensive when you question their commitment or the sincerity of their remorse. They really just want you to leave them alone and let them get back to the business of eating cake.

So let's recap. Why do cheaters cheat? For kibbles. What's the best way to ensure kibble production is robust? Cake (having both the spouse and the affair partners). How do cheaters stay in cake? Through an insidious kind of manipulation I refer to as the **"pick me" dance**. The cheater doesn't have to demand cake from you, oh no. They'll provoke you into a competition in which you're begging to give it to them.

The Humiliating Dance of "Pick Me!"

One of the most common mindfucks chumps may experience after discovery of an affair, is the expectation that they will try harder to win back the cheater. This expectation either comes from the cheater directly— "I cheated because you're a lousy (partner, housekeeper, lay)"— and how are you going to up your game to keep me? Or it comes from the dependency of the chump—"What did I do to make him cheat? And how can I be a better partner to make him stay?" Often both dynamics are at play, and feed into each other. The cheater, of course, is quite happy to pin this shit on you.

When terrible things happen, it's very natural to want to feel a sense of control. To think, oh if I'd only done X, Y would not have resulted. If you are at fault, the reasoning goes, well, then you could fix this. (Chumps love to fix things.) So you will take this crappy situation, and think you can control the outcome by just trying harder.

This is a bad idea for several reasons. First, you aren't at fault for another's cheating. That's on them. As they say in therapy about people behaving self destructively—the Three C Rule—"you didn't **cause** it, you cannot **cure** it, and you cannot **control** it."

Second, if you see the affair as a competition that you must try harder to "win," the marriage becomes a bidding war between the chump and the affair partner. The best response is to fold, because the game is rigged. There is no winning bid. The cheater just wants the competition to go on indefinitely. They want to sit impassively while you do the humiliating dance of "pick me!" This makes them feel powerful and special.

Cheating comes from a sense of entitlement. All you do when you compete for your marriage is solidify that entitlement—that it is *your* job to ensure the happiness of the cheater, and hey, you missed a spot. Healthy relationships are based upon reciprocity. Infidelity is a toxically lopsided situation. Cheaters want the scales tipped in their favor (more attention, more ego stroking, more sex, more materialism) at your expense. They just don't want to try that hard, and they're gonna sulk if you make them.

What does the humiliating dance of "pick me!" look like?

- Mounting a defense of the marriage—trying to hard sell your cheater on What You Have Together.

- Eating the shit sandwich. Not bringing up the affair. Stuffing your emotions so as not to upset the cheater with your distress.

- Believing that the cheater's need for "happiness" is paramount to the commitment they made to you. If they want to break that commitment, fine, there are honest ways to do that, beginning with a divorce lawyer. If they want to work on happiness, there is therapy, God, and working at pet shelters. But they cannot have all the benefits of marriage and a side dish fuck because they aren't "happy."

- Let's make a deal! Don't make a bargain with the Devil—as long as you try harder to make the cheater happy and fix what's wrong, they won't betray you.

- Super spouse! Having hysterical bonding sex, going to the gym, and dressing spiffier. If you're trying to be a better you to "win," you're just rewarding them. Be a better you for you. (Your next partner will appreciate it a lot more than they will.)

The pick me dance is doomed to failure, because again, it's predicated on the cheater's sense of entitlement—that your marriage is a contest instead of a commitment. If you dance you're legitimating the idea that you somehow caused the cheating, or can reverse course to back to your favor. You have an illusion of control (I can win this!), but in reality your cheater calls the dance tune.

Stop the music. Your *cheater* broke the commitment. Assuming that such a grievous betrayal can be remedied, the repair work is done through humility *not entitlement*. You are worth more than the pick me polka. Hang up your dance shoes.

Chapter 4

Stupid Shit Cheaters Say – And How to Respond

"I didn't betray you by cheating, I betrayed your belief that I would not cheat."

—An actual Stupid Shit Cheaters Say submission at chumplady.com

Cheaters say the darndest things.

Chumps are usually just so gobsmacked at the excuses cheaters give, that we remain silently agog, or sputter in disbelief. Or worse, we try to mount a defense against the crazy talk, coming away from such encounters feeling mentally scrambled, like we stuck our heads in a blender.

Haven't you wanted the perfect rejoinder? Wouldn't you love to know what's going on inside their noggins to make them spout such nonsense?

Well, wonder no more. Here's your guide to stupid shit cheaters say—and how to respond.

One caveat—don't use this to try and match wits with your cheater. That's pointless. You may as well try and shame a doorpost. Instead think of this as a Field Guide to Idiocy. Oh look, a yellow-bellied bullshitter! Must be mating season.

If you can identify the mindfuckery, you can disarm it. The responses given here are not to engage with the cheater, or to try and achieve a consensus that yes, they suck. The responses are for you to **assert yourself** and **put that blame right back squarely where it belongs**—on the cheater.

I love you but I'm not in love with you.

A classic. Translated it means—"I did unloving things, but telling you 'I love you' makes me feel better about them." I love you but I'm not in love with you is simply impression management.

It has nothing to do with you, chumps. This is about maintaining the cheater's self image. And it softens the blow—hey, you wouldn't impose consequences on someone who **loves** you, would you? They think they're letting you down gently.

Cheater love is a compartmentalized kind of love—"I love you, but I put that aside while I was fucking someone else." The two things aren't at all connected. Why should "love" get in the way of a good time?

Chumps naively assume that people who love us *act* like they love us. Cheaters subvert that assumption and turn it back on chumps. "But I'm not *in love* with you" is a subtle blameshift. "I don't feel giddy and effervescent. I need sparkles. Alas, if you had only twinkled brighter, perhaps it would not have come to this." It's so disappointing the way you've let them down. What can you do to make it up to them?

"I love you, but I'm not in love with you" is your cue to perform the pick me dance. They may be dumping you anyway for the affair partner, but some parting kibbles would be nice.

The subtle mindfuck of "I love you but I'm not in love with you" is that it's not definitive. It's pure **cake speak**. They aren't saying, "Hey, I love someone else. It's over. I'm sorry." No, there is an opening—they *love you*. Just not in that way.

It's a deliberate confusion, this whole torn between two lovers schtick. It keeps the cheater in cake and kibbles, and makes their desires central. The cheater can feel very noble about their love for you in the face of your inadequacies. They'd like credit for that higher sentiment—but they're unburdened by their commitments because King's X!—they're not *in love* with you.

To a cheater "I'm not *in love* with you" is a justifiable reason for casting about and loving someone else. So, which came first? The falling out of love, or the permission they gave themselves to cast about?

We all know grown-up love means not feeling "in love" all the livelong day. There are no butterflies when you're doing taxes, or visiting the in-laws, or cleaning up after a kid's stomach flu.

Response

Chumps, don't try to parse with your cheater which parts of you they love or what their butterflies are saying to them today—state what **you** need.

"I need to be in a relationship where I am fully loved and respected. You don't love me the way I deserve to be loved. Buh-BYE." Don't ask yourself what you did to be so unlovable. Don't dance the pick me dance. Just let them go. I'm sure their butterflies will be migrating again soon.

I didn't intend to hurt you.

Hurting you was unintentional? Cheating is about as deliberate as a NATO airstrike. There's nothing unintentional about secret cell phones, dating profiles, diverted monies, and clandestine hook-ups. It takes a lot of planning and premeditation to cheat. What was unintentional was you finding out about it.

Cheaters prefer the passive voice language of "mistakes were made" after discovery. (No pronouns, no responsibility!) In the real world, people don't just accidently land on each other's genitals. It's not a "mistake" or something that "just happened." That sort of language distances cheaters from personal responsibility for their crappy choices.

"I didn't intend to hurt you" is gaslighting with some blameshifting thrown in for good measure. Hey, hurting you wasn't a *conscious* choice. If you want to *interpret* what I did as hurtful, well, that's on you. But it's not how I *intended* it. See how this trick works? The onus shifts from the cheater (who didn't intend to hurt you) to you (a person who has mistakenly taken offense where offense wasn't intended). Left out of the equation is that they did something offensive.

"I didn't intend to hurt you" is another gem of impression management. Yes, they are cheaters, but not Bad People. It's not like they go around feeling like Dr. Evil, plotting your downfall. Hurting you was completely beside the point! You're a bit of collateral damage, that's all; so don't take it so hard. What's important to remember is that the cheater is still a Splendid Person. (See also "I loved you all along.")

The fact is **they didn't care if they hurt you**. Not enough. They did the risk benefit analysis and fucking around won out over your feelings every time.

Response

"I don't care about your intentions. They're irrelevant. You knew full well that cheating on me would hurt me, which is why you kept it a secret. You didn't intend to hurt me? Well, you didn't intentionally try to keep me from harm either."

You weren't meeting my needs.

Another variant is "I haven't been happy for a long time." Well, news to you, I'm sure. Has your happiness been off the charts? I didn't think so, and yet you managed to keep it in your pants. Funny that.

"You weren't meeting my needs" is more blameshifting. The cheater was compelled to cheat because of something lacking in you, versus something lacking in them—character.

By putting the focus on you and your inadequacies, it takes the focus off their infidelities. Pay no attention to that gut-wrenching betrayal! Let's discuss your inability to make dark coffee!

I know the reasons given are usually not as frivolous as that. (But sometimes they are. You should see my mail.) Usually they're far more intimate and cutting like you're bad in bed, you spend too much time with the children, or you work too much.

You might own your faults. You might rack your brain for the thousand examples of loving things you did for your cheater to demonstrate your worthiness. **Please stop**. This isn't about you. You didn't drive anyone to cheat. Look, if you had the superpower to compel other people do things, do you think you would choose to be cheated on? This shit is completely on them.

If they were unhappy in the marriage, there are honest conversations, marriage counselors, or divorce lawyers. They didn't choose those options—they cheated.

Some therapists like to peddle the notion that affairs happen because of "unmet needs." That's nonsense. Affairs happen because of lousy character. Perhaps some would argue that these are not mutually exclusive notions—the cheater had unmet needs, but just went about meeting them in unethical ways. (Like I have an unmet need to be rich, and so I rob banks.)

It would be much more productive if we challenged cheaters about the plausibility of their needs, and the "happiness" that is an ever-moving goal post. At whose expense are cheaters "meeting their needs"? Why are these needs a secret and not communicated? Is it because they are timid forest creatures who cannot express themselves? Or is it simply that honesty gets in the way of the Ashley Madison profiles?

My cheating ex had a "need" to lead a double life as a serial cheater. I did not meet that need, as I cannot be a smorgasbord of pussy. My bad.

Response

Don't accept responsibility for their cheating.

"You weren't meeting my needs either, and I didn't cheat on you. Please don't try and pawn this crap off on me."

I need time to decide.

No they do not. This is not "Let's Make a Deal." I need time to decide is a stalling tactic for cake.

Chumps have a hard time understanding the concept of cake. We think it's really a contest between the affair partner(s) and us. Cheaters, however, want to maximize kibble production and prefer a situation in which they've got you and the affair partner(s) competing for their awesomeness. They may tell you they're trying to decide between you all, and plead for patience, *it's just so difficult*, but really they're reveling in cake.

There you are stomping your foot, threatening cake loss. This is unacceptable. So the cheater will put you off with delay tactics. They'll take your chump temperature—how sympathetic are you to their plight? Will you dance the pick me dance? Will you understand that, hey, they're grieving too? This is very hard, you know. They might ask for a separation, which is really just permission for unbridled cake without you around to monitor their whereabouts.

Remember, **your marriage is not a contest**. You have no obligation to stick around while your cheater vacillates like Hamlet without his Ritalin. No one's got time for that.

Staying "in it to win it" means you've already lost. This isn't marriage, it's a rigged game to keep your cheater in cake.

Response

"You can't decide if you want to be married to me? I am not a consolation prize. I am your spouse. This isn't a bidding war and I'm not going to compete for the honor of your ambivalence. There's the door. I'm getting on with my life without you."

We could have an open marriage. Monogamy isn't natural.

It's one thing to begin with an open marriage. It's quite another to have it thrust upon you after the discovery of an affair. This "offer" is not sexual sophistication, it's an implied threat—let me have my cake, or we're through. The cheater lays the blame with monogamy—that impossible condition that, oh hey, we all agreed to.

The problem isn't monogamy. The problem is that the cheater unilaterally changed the terms of the marriage agreement.

You are presented with a choice now, which at least is out in the open. Agree to let your spouse have multiple partners, and you can enjoy the same, or end the relationship.

If you accept the open arrangement, you would need to negotiate the sort of terms that polyamorists set, such as, am I the primary relationship? Who is an acceptable partner? Can we ask mutual friends? How much time is spent on extracurriculars? How do we manage risk for STDs, etc.?

But the problem there is you'd be negotiating relationship terms with someone who just demonstrated to you that they couldn't be trusted. They behave unilaterally and change the terms of agreed upon arrangements (like monogamous marriage). Open relationships are based on trust too.

So what do *you* want? Do you want a monogamous relationship? If so, stand up for that.

Response

"I'm not going to get sidetracked with a discussion about how natural monogamy is. You agreed to monogamy, and let me play by those rules, and changed them for yourself. That's a matter of character, not monogamy. If you don't wish to be monogamous, I appreciate your candor. I do want a monogamous relationship. We're incompatible."

I don't understand your hostility.

Cheaters can be an exceptionally dimwitted bunch. When it comes to connecting the dots between their actions and devastating outcomes, they get a little confused about the fuss. File this one under: "The problem isn't what I did, it's your reaction to it."

Apparently, you aren't taking this betrayal in quite the way they expected. I mean, not that they gave a lot of thought to you finding out, but now that you have, they imagined you'd be a bit more... well, *chill*. Where is all this crazy anger coming from? Of course they'd like to talk to you about it, but you're making that impossible with your emotional overreactions. They don't like the tone of your voice, and this isn't a very convenient time right now. Maybe when you can calm down.

No. That's still not calm enough. No. They detect judgment. Try again later when you can speak in a civil tone. Or really... don't bother.

"I don't understand your hostility" is gaslighting. It's minimizing abuse, as if to say "there's nothing here to be upset about, but I'm glad *someone* can be the adult here."

Denying reality is a recipe to drive anyone stark raving bonkers. Of course, such mindfuckery only makes you more "hostile," which is the very pretext not to speak with you.

When you get righteously angry with a cheater, you've upset the power balance. They miss that sweet spot when you were in the dark and they could do whatever they wanted to. Now that you know, and you're pissed, the cheater needs to reassert their superiority and control. It takes some brass balls to pretend they have no idea why you're upset, but hey, the best defense is a good offense.

Response

"You don't understand my hostility? Let your lawyer explain it to you after I have you served. He bills in 6-minute increments. Hope you're a quick study."

But I loved you all along.

Nothing confuses a chump more than hearing that their cheater truly loved them the entire time they were cheating on them. The heartbroken chump wants to believe it, but it does sound rather impossible.

Instead of "cheating on you," let's substitute the words "pushed you down a flight of stairs" and see if sounds less ridiculous.

"I know I pushed you down a flight of stairs, honey, but all the time I was watching you flail about, hitting the landing, and breaking your collarbone, I was loving you. Truly."

Are you buying it? As anyone who has experienced infidelity knows, the pain of betrayal is far worse than the physical pain of bouncing head first down a flight of stairs. Could someone who risked your safety and emotional well-being for a thrill be described as "loving" you right then? No.

But it's a common trope that cheaters "never stopped loving you." And chumps go through all sorts of mental contortions to make these two incongruous things—loving and cheating—fit together.

"Okay, I loved you. But in this kind of familiar way, like you love a brother, or an old pair of jeans, or a really annoying roommate, sort of thing. But I was always in love with you."

This ability to "love" you while cheating on you is often attributed to "compartmentalization." Yes, I loved you. But then I was able to shelf it just long enough to fuck that other guy and put my wedding ring in my pocket. When I came home, shazzam! I loved you again.

It's like "love" is this background noise cheaters claim they feel the whole time. But it apparently isn't a strong enough force to not make them cheat in the first place.

"I never stopped loving you" is something that cheaters like to tell themselves, to make themselves out to be Not So Bad.

Betrayal is unloving. You cannot cheat without rationalizations. Cheaters construct narratives as to why they deserve an affair and why you should be kept in the dark. Whatever the cheater wants—side dish fucks, ego kibbles, unfettered access to money—trumps the well-being of the chump.

If the cheater has to hurt you to get those kibbles (i.e., push you down a flight of stairs), they would do it. They risk the consequences (which they think will never happen) and are indifferent to your pain.

Real love is about connection. You have to be emotionally and spiritually disconnected from someone to be able to cheat on them.

For a cheater to say, "yes, I did **not** love you then, I callously betrayed you," would be the truth. And that is a lot harder for a chump to overcome than the cheater copping to the lesser offense that they behaved badly, but "always loved you."

Can they love you again after betraying you? I suppose it is possible. But you forever have to live with the knowledge that this person is capable of pushing you down a flight of stairs (betraying you) to get what they want. It's very difficult to feel safe again in that sort of relationship.

Response

"I don't believe you loved me while you were cheating on me. Love and betrayal are incompatible. I don't feel safe with that kind of 'love.'"

If you met him/her—you'd really them! He/she's a lot like you!

Of all the stupid shit cheaters say, this is among the more patently moronic. Oh yeah, if this person wasn't fucking your spouse, you could be *best friends*.

Besides the obvious insult—do you really think I have less moral sense than God gave dryer lint?—it's propaganda to convince you that the affair partner is a Really Good Person. Why would your cheater assert something so ridiculous? Because they're minimizing. Hey, the cheater is a good person, the affair partner is a good person. They're all just good people caught up in something larger than them both. Where is your compassion? This person is *just like you*. Someone you could really like if you'd get over your prejudice.

"You'd like them!" says a lot about your cheater's narcissistic world view. You're all just interchangeable really, united in your love for the cheater. One's as good as the next, but what matters here are the kibbles. Wouldn't it be great if you were all friends together supplying the cheater kibbles? A cake fantasy come to life!

Response

"I'm nothing like your fuckbuddy. I don't sleep around with married people."

I would try to reconcile, but you're never going to forgive me.

Yep, your inability to forgive is the real problem here. Notice how the focus is not on the cheater stepping up to demonstrate remorse, but on the chump having to prove their fealty to the cheater. Yet another example of "the problem is not what I did, it's your reaction to it."

"You're never going to forgive me" is an invitation to do the pick me dance. What are you supposed to say? "Oh yes! I'm certain I could forgive you! Just give me this chance to try, please!" As your guts are spilled out all over the floor and you want die from grief? It's pure mindfuckery. At this moment of all moments, you are supposed to reassure *them*?

Essentially, the cheater is saying, "I'm not going to try unless you give me a guarantee." Isn't that nice? More entitlement. They'd like a risk-free investment. But you there, saddled with a cheater, what you have at stake is irrelevant.

Any cheater who can utter these words has absolutely zero interest in sincerely reconciling with you. True reconciliation, that rare unicorn, is based on humility. A repentant cheater must assume the risk that you won't get over it, you won't find it in your heart to forgive, but they will make that Herculean effort regardless. True remorse does not come from a place of entitlement.

So why would they say such a thing? Because then they can leave and you're cast as the bad guy. The quitter. The person who wasn't trying hard enough. The cheater is the poor sausage, the victim of your warrantless bad opinion. If you couldn't forgive, hey, it's all on you.

Response

"What makes you think you're entitled to reconciliation or my forgiveness?"

I need to mourn the end of the affair.

Oh hell to the NO. Of all the pernicious entitlements, this one rises to the top. The argument goes that cheaters, when they end an affair (or more likely, are dumped), are in a state of withdrawal. It's a real "loss" and if you're a good spouse, you'll help them through it. Pass a hanky, be a shoulder to cry on. If you can't manage that, you churlish chump, the least you can do is understand that they're "grieving."

I'm not saying cheaters don't mourn the end of their covert fuckfests. I'm sure the loss of cake is utterly tragic. What I'm saying is why should you give a flip? You're mourning too—your marriage as you knew it, the loss of trust, your sense of personal safety—and the difference is this nightmare was inflicted on you. Your losses are not equivalent. What your cheater is suffering is completely self-inflicted. It's like the story of the man who kills his parents and then wants clemency from the court for being an orphan.

It is the worst kind of delusional grandiosity to expect that the person you grievously harmed be the same person to comfort you.

When I hit you in the head with that hammer, I cut my hand. Will you bring me a band-aid and kiss my boo boo?

We would think such a scenario ridiculous, and yet there are therapists out there who encourage chumps to accept this affair loss "grief" and be sympathetic. Why? Because they don't see affairs as decisions—like say, hitting a person in the head with a hammer. That's so overtly unkind! Unlike fucking around and risking a person's health, which hey, is just a thing that happens with no aforethought whatsoever.

Response

You mourn the affair partner? You mourn alone.

"Get out of my house. Go sit shiva on your affair somewhere else. It's not my job to comfort you from the affliction of your own stupidity. I've got my own healing to do, which apparently isn't even on your radar. Fuck off!"

⁓ ⁓

Now, if you're still in the throes of chumpdom, I'm sure you're reading this chapter thinking, "Gee Chump Lady, you're a little harsh. I mean, maybe they'll come out of the fog eventually and I'm going to scare them off with all this anger! And I'll miss my chance for a true reconciliation because I hurt their feelings during a time of great confusion."

If a cheater is confused, that's not your problem to fix. Any attempt to end their "confusion" is a form of the pick me dance. You cannot nice anyone out of an affair. You can only draw boundaries and enforce those boundaries and the first boundary chumps must enforce is refusing to accept responsibility for the cheater's actions. They shift that blame? You dump it right back on 'em.

There can be no reconciliation where there is entitlement thinking. True remorse and entitlement cannot coexist. Every example given of stupid shit cheaters say is mired in narcissism. If you've heard any of these utterances and this same cheater wants to reconcile with you? They want to keep eating cake. Close the bakery and get on with your life, pronto.

CHAPTER 5

Reconciliation – Am I a Unicorn?

"Patience is a minor form of despair, disguised as a virtue."

—*Kazi Nazrul Islam*

So you're reading this survival guide to infidelity, but what you may want to know is—can my marriage be saved? Because even though you might recognize a lot of the mindfuckery, and are righteously upset about it, you'd prefer to be exceptional. Let this cup of motherfucking pain pass me by. Please God let me be one of the lucky people whose marriages survive and are made stronger by infidelity.

If I had a better head for business, I could make a lot of money fanning your false hopes. (Being a bucket of cold water tends not to be a winning sales strategy.) A quick Google search will turn up any number of snake oil salesmen who will affair-proof your marriage for $399. These people sell the seductive idea that you alone can control this. All it takes is your heroic patience to save your marriage. No problem if your cheater's not onboard! Stay the course! Stand for your marriage! Make it a good place to be! Wait for the fog to clear! Buy another motivational DVD!

The problem with these "save your marriage" bozos is that they work from the assumption that either you can single-handedly control the outcome of your marriage, or that your cheater is totally onboard, demonstrates remorse, and is committed to fixing the relationship. That's like selling you a book on "How to Be a Millionaire" and the first step is to have $999,999 in the bank. It's exceedingly rare to have a fully committed cheater at D-Day (obviously, or they would not have cheated on you).

What the Reconciliation Industrial Complex doesn't tell you is what to do in the very likely situation your cheater is on the fence, doesn't seem as sorry as they should be, and wants to blame this whole mess on you. At Chump Lady the question isn't how can you work with that—but *why would you want to?*

Writing a happy ending to the infidelity nightmare is an alluring notion. If we are the problem, we've got the power to fix that! And isn't that selling chumps more of the codependency to which we are already prone—that we can control people through our actions? *If I'm just good enough, then you'll be good.* And the ugly flipside—that we are responsible for other people's behavior. *I was bad. I drove you to this. I made you hurt me.*

No one possesses superpowers that compel other people to do things. You can't save a marriage by yourself any more than you can bend steel with your mind, or levitate avocados through positive thinking. Sorry, the success or failure of your marriage doesn't rest with you alone. That's at once liberating and terrifying. You only control yourself, that's it.

So when you team up with a cheater, and remain teamed up, **you still only control you**. If your cheater is intent on driving their life into a ditch, no one—shrink, author, or motivational speaker—can compel your cheater to behave differently or give them a character transplant. Reconciliation is a crapshoot because it depends on factors you don't control—your cheater's investment in the process. You're making a bet on a person who has demonstrated that they are a bad risk. You can either add to your sunk costs and maybe your stock will rise again, or you can quit investing.

You might risk reconciliation because of faith and wishful thinking—*my cheater is going to discover a newfound appreciation for monogamy and me!*—or you might risk reconciliation with a cool appraisal of your existing reality, noting how demonstrably sorry your cheater behaves and how strong your boundaries are and how adept you are at enforcing them.

But whatever you do, let go of the idea that being cheated on serves some higher purpose in your marriage. That's hogwash. Infidelity strengthens marriage the same way shooting off your kneecaps improves your tennis game. Which is to say, it doesn't. It's a calamitous injury. And to think that such an assault is improving is the worst kind of nonsense. Would we say such a thing about physical abuse? *Being headbutted into a doorway was really the best thing that ever happened to my marriage! Ever since Bob took those anger management courses, we're so much closer!* Of course that's crap. But hooking up for bareback sex with strangers on Craigslist is some how less injurious?

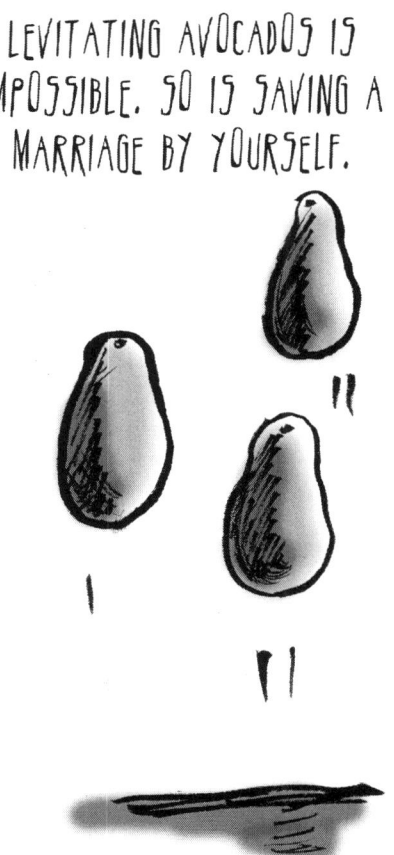

Infidelity destroys trust and obliterates your sense of personal safety. It endangers your health, your children's home-life, your finances, and your sanity. After being cheated on, your marriage might endure, it might limp, but it sure as hell isn't going to skip the light fandango. You will always live with the knowledge that this person betrayed you. That never goes away. As I like to say, "You can't unring that bell or unfuck that whore."

Of course, the trope goes that you'll rebuild. With a lot of hard work, you'll forget and forgive the injury in time. Theoretically, I think that is *possible*. I just don't think it is *probable*. I liken successful reconciliation to a unicorn—a mythical creature that I want to believe in, but which is rarely sighted.

So why am I skeptical about reconciliation? **Entitlement**.

Infidelity is a choice. People cheat because they feel entitled to cheat. That's it. That's my simple answer to the painful question of **why**? I don't believe people cheat because they're broken, or their FOO issues, or because of the staggering powers of Facebook crushes. I don't believe people cheat because of mid-life crises, which descend on former church deacons like a toxic cloud of musk cologne. I don't believe people cheat because of perimenopause. I don't believe people cheat because that hussy flung herself at him and wore down his defenses after his mother died. I don't believe people cheat because they lost 20 pounds and got a new haircut. I don't believe people cheat because monogamy is not an evolutionary imperative. I believe people cheat because **they give themselves permission to cheat**—and that's a matter of character.

So when D-Day hits, it does rather beggar belief that this person is going to lead with humility. To do that, they'd have to call into question their entitlement. And let's face it, entitlement feels awesome. Humility, not so much.

Entitlement, of course, only feels awesome if you can suppress empathy. (Truly disordered people do not do empathy.) Entitlement is—all the cookies for me! Empathy is—well, maybe I should share my cookies. You look sad without a cookie. As much as I *want* all the cookies, I don't know if I can enjoy my cookies knowing that you're sad not having a cookie.

When people are caught cheating they do a lot of things to keep entitlement alive. They gaslight. *Cookies? I don't have cookies.* They blameshift. *It is Right and Proper that I have all the cookies, because you don't know how to appreciate cookies.* They mindfuck. *I would give you a cookie, but I was thinking of your health. You can't handle sugar.* They obfuscate. *Cookie? Define cookie.*

As long as there is entitlement, there is no hope at reconciliation.

Once you realize that, everything else falls into place. Chumps tie themselves in knots on the transparency issue. She didn't give me her passwords! He won't close his Facebook account! How can I monitor this?

You don't have to. The fact that they feel **entitled** to their privacy means this is a nonstarter. They feel **entitled** to not answer your questions. They feel **entitled** to keep working with the person. They feel **entitled** to keep their good opinion of the affair partner alive.

The biggest, most humungous entitlement I see after discovery is that cheaters feel **entitled to reconciliation**, period. They think they deserve all the time they want to come out of the "fog." To answer your questions. To read a book, or schedule a shrink appointment. They feel grossly entitled to a chump's patience.

Moreover, they feel entitled to all the marital perks they enjoyed before discovery of their affairs. Comfort and validation from the chump. Sex. Housework. Income.

Humility is much harder. Humility means that it's not all about you. It means you manage your expectations of any reward. Humility accepts consequences and lets go of outcomes. Humility does not try to control the narrative or protect its image.

Humility is painful. It wrestles with shame. Humility recognizes that regaining trust is a long, slow process that may end, despite their best efforts. Humility works hard without pay. Humility is forthcoming. Humility doesn't keep secrets.

Most chumps who desire reconciliation accept that transforming entitlement into humility is a process. And so, after being betrayed, wrestling with their own enormous grief, chumps accept yet *more* humility and eat shit sandwiches waiting for their cheaters to catch up on this humility thing.

But cheaters are often very slow learners. There are false starts and failures at no contact. They "grieve" the affair partner, staring blankly at questions they "don't remember." Very few cheaters do humility right out of the starting gate, if ever.

Chumps put a lot of stock in humility, because they're so good at it. They believe their cheaters will come around. They put faith in those displays of regret, tears, and apologies. Chumps stay the course, because they believe in the **transformative powers of pain**. Surely, this person will see how much they hurt me and will feel moved to fix this. Chumps also believe that the cheater's *own* pain will make them connect the dots of action to consequence.

But ask yourself—who are those tears really for? The chump, or for the cheater who fears consequences? Not every cheater is a sociopathic monster unable to feel empathy, but every cheater is a known manipulator. So be skeptical before you buy into their remorse. Consider under what conditions are people who have demonstrated poor character motivated to change?

True change is a long process that requires delayed gratification. What is the likelihood that is an attractive course of action for cheaters?

Why would someone prone to escapism—an affair—mature into someone capable of delayed gratification? Why would someone high on entitlement choose the painful path of humility? The rewards of character development are not immediate and they're humbling. The biggest reward for cheaters choosing reconciliation is the absence of tangible consequences (loss of income versus the loss of respect, which is intangible). Chumps believe cheaters will stay in line because there's so much to lose—one's family and finances and the respect of the children!

But cheaters don't think they're in danger of losing that. Why not? *Because you're still there.* Helping them with their homework, loving them through it, holding their hand on this humility thing. Reconciliation itself does not help cheaters with their entitlement issues. If anything, it hurts authentic progress because it doesn't level meaningful consequences.

But they'll be so grateful you gave them that chance! Will they? Or will they feel entitled to it? After suffering my own series of false reconciliations, reading years on infidelity boards, and running my own blog, I've yet to see the grateful, prodigal unicorn. Instead I see refugees from failed reconciliations, some many years after the original affair. Think about it—if cheaters valued how much you've done for them, do you think they would disrespect you with an affair to begin with? It's hard to appreciate that which you feel is unconditionally yours. And even if cheaters do feel a true sense of gratitude for another chance—can they kill off entitlement thinking altogether?

"Reformed" cheaters can be like dry drunks—all the entitlement, without the sexual acting out. They may spend more of the marital assets, do less housework, not work a regular job, engage in immature behavior, and blameshift. Why? Because they still retain the belief that they're special. The advantageous lopsidedness works for them. *You* are fortunate to have the wonderfulness that is *them*. You wind up the responsible, resented parent to their willful, indulged child. Is that a relationship worth saving?

If you were a cheater examining your choices after D-Day, what would be your most likely choice? Let's play out the options:

Authentic reconciliation—Shame and mortification, hard work of rebuilding trust without guaranteed reward, but you get to keep your marriage, family, and finances intact. Eternally having to express gratitude to your chump for taking you back could create a weird power dynamic, but is probably essential.

Cake (false reconciliation)—The veneer of reconciliation, doing the bare minimum in terms of apologies and marriage counseling. No shame, no mortification (because the chump won't tell anyone and will continue to protect your image). Marriage, family, and finances intact. And options remain open for current or future affairs.

Escape—Follow the trail of stardust and leave for your sparkly affair partner. Okay, you lose the marriage, family, and half the finances, but you gain sparkles and there is some imaginary trading up. If you remain "friends" with your ex, you may be able to control the narrative. The escape option also keeps cake alive—you may scout for a new hypotenuse for your triangle.

Divorce—Consequences. No marriage, half time with family (if that), half the finances. Mortification, shame, no controlling the chump's narrative. But a chance to start over with a clean slate and someone new.

The only two honest choices here are **authentic reconciliation** and **divorce**—the two hardest paths. If you're a person with demonstrated poor character, which path do you think would be most tempting? If you're prone to escapism and entitlement—how long do you think you can stay on a hard path without lapsing? Only one of these paths requires total humility—reconciliation. The other three let you keep most or all of your cookies.

See why I'm skeptical?

The difference between real remorse and genuine imitation Naugahyde remorse

The problem with reconciliation isn't just residual entitlement either; often the problem is chumps themselves who see remorse where it doesn't really exist. (We'll get to chumps and "spackle" ability in the next chapter.) Chumps are so invested in controlling this scary outcome, that they chase unicorns. "I think I see a glimmer of insight!" "He says he's sorry!" "She told me she just needs a little more time, but I can't scare her off with my demands!"

So how do you tell if you've got something to work with? Start judging your cheater by their actions. **Sorry is as sorry does**.

Is it real remorse? Or is it genuine imitation Naugahyde remorse (GINR)? You know, sort of looks like the real thing, but upon closer inspection is a cheap fake. Here's a handy checklist to help you distinguish.

1. **Humility**. Cheating is about entitlement. Being truly sorry is about humility. That means the cheater doesn't go first in anything for a long time, such as airing their grievances about the marriage, or putting their demands for "closure" with the affair partner above a spouse's healing. (Grieving the affair partner? Not on your time.) Remorse is the cheater recognizing their place on the food chain as the Person Who Fucked Up—not the Poor Misunderstood Sausage. That means a chump's

grief is not met with dismissive anger. That means there are no false equivalencies. (Well, you make mistakes too!) True remorse is a deep awareness that infidelity broke a sacred trust, and the cheater is not owed reconciliation.

2. **Initiative**. Real remorse books its own shrink appointments. Real remorse does the homework. Real remorse does not need to be cajoled, wheedled, or dragged by its ear. Real remorse buys the books and *reads* the books. GINR waits for you to do it, and then finds a very good reason to be too busy.

3. **Honesty**. You can't cheat on someone without lying to them. Real remorse spits out the truth. *All* of the truth, and it doesn't editorialize and say things like "she really needed me" or "he was just a friend." Real remorse answers the same questions over and over and over again and gives truthful, consistent answers. (None of which is "I don't know.") If real remorse doesn't know, real remorse does whatever it can to find out. Real remorse doesn't balk at a polygraph. GINR thinks polygraphs are expensive and unreliable. Real remorse would stand on its head wearing a tutu if it gave you peace of mind, even if real remorse thinks your request is kind of stupid.

4. **Patience**. Real remorse understands that repairing a relationship after infidelity is a long haul with dubious prospects. GINR wants you to "get over it" already because hey, it *said it was sorry*.

5. **Ownership**. See Humility. Real remorse wears the shame. Real remorse takes responsibility for the fallout. Real remorse is okay if you tell people, because you need the support. GINR wants you to protect its image. GINR blameshifts and says "we all brought issues to this marriage that led me to cheat." GINR minimizes and obfuscates.

6. **Recompense**. Real remorse understands that reconciliation is a risky investment. GINR wants you to assume all that risk and how dare you ask for any assurances, because *don't you trust me?* Real remorse runs a credit report on itself and shows you. Real remorse puts its money where its mouth is with a post-nup with an infidelity clause. A completely useless document if the cheater never cheats again, which of course, only the cheater has control over. Real remorse pays your legal bill. Real remorse compensates you and your children for every dime spent on the

affair(s). Real remorse recognizes that there are financial and time losses as real as the emotional ones. Time and heartbreak cannot be recompensed. Money can. Real remorse says, it's the least I can do.

I'm feeling lucky! I believe in unicorns.

Remember regardless of remorse (or genuine imitation Naugahyde remorse) you don't owe anybody reconciliation. If cheating is a deal breaker for you, it's a deal breaker. You didn't break your vows and you're perfectly within your rights to walk, even if your cheater desperately wants another chance. Understanding that, and letting you walk away is part of demonstrating true remorse. (Guilting you or calling you a quitter is the sign of an asshole.)

Generally, however, it's a minority of chumps who walk away from a remorseful cheater. Most of us get the other kind—the not-totally-on-board, or up-and-left sort of cheaters. Yet given a chance, most of us try reconciliation at least for a while. Chumps have big hearts.

We often tell our cheaters—okay, you get this one come-to-Jesus chance, but *next* time, I'm going to impose those consequences! Be afraid! (Newsflash: they are not afraid, because they don't believe you. Why don't they believe you? Because you're still there.)

Chumps think that cheaters fear consequences, and if we just keep them on a short enough leash, or threaten the loss of their family and finances, they will tow the line—and then here is the really absurd part—grow to love us again. But think about it—do you want a person you have to hold a legal gun to their head to get them to commit to you? Do you want someone you have to leave before they recognize your worth? How many times will you have to dump them, or threaten to dump them, to slap some sense into their heads? Does that sound at all sustainable?

What evidence do you have that they will truly recommit to you, other than hope? Do you really want to be someone's consolation prize? Or worse, the marriage police?

This is the sticky wicket—if you don't "trust but verify" then you just trust them. Trusting them is how you got blindsided. It's very difficult to feel safe in a marriage where you keep expecting the bottom to drop out, or keep hypervigilant to ensure that it doesn't.

My advice to you is to get on with your new life. Let your cheater improve their character on their own time. Your time is precious. They are a dubious prospect and you need to see much better returns over time before you invest in their stock.

If they are truly sorry, they will do the hard work on themselves regardless of what you do. Cheaters often cast their investment in reconciliation as something that is completely chump-dependent. They want guarantees. "Well, I suppose I'll try if you don't quit on me." Pretty rich coming from the person who quit the marriage, huh? Chumps think cheaters need this handholding to come around. If you're in this situation, it's already doomed because your cheater is blameshifting their lack of commitment on to you. They need to do the heavy lifting, and not pass the mess over to your side. If a cheater gets their shit together, hey, they know where to find you.

It's hard to believe it now, but there is a better life on the other side of this crazy. Consider your other options. Monogamy is not 12-step. Some people actually keep their commitments. Their words align with their actions. There are folks who will cherish and respect you. Wouldn't you rather be with one of those souls than this reclamation project?

I think you can do better. I know you deserve better.

CHAPTER 6

Chumps, Why Are You Stuck?

"I've learned from my mistakes and I'm sure I can repeat them exactly."

—*Peter Cook*

So you've just read my polemic about why reconciliation is a risky endeavor with bad odds, and you've either concluded hmm… I've got a point, or I'm a bitter cheerleader for divorce who wants you to grow old alone in a bunker full of cats.

I promise Chump Lady is a nice person who wants better for you. It's not that I think divorce is a picnic, it's that I know there is a better life waiting for you on the other side of this mess. If I'm cheerleading anything, it's that you leave a remorseless cheater and arrive at your new life with your soul intact.

You may have a gut feeling that your relationship is unsustainable. Heck, you may have mountains of evidence that your relationship is unsustainable. In fact, your cheater may have already left the building or proposed "separation" (read: unfettered access to cake), and you're conflicted about letting go. Or perhaps you're on your umpteenth round of reconciliation, hoping against hope that *this* time your cheater really means it and is going to commit to you. Or maybe this is your first D-Day and you're confused, but don't want to be a quitter. (Except in those dark

hours when you feel like, yes! yes! lay this burden down!) Yet as shattered as you are, you probably still love this person. It's hard to leave someone you're so invested in.

This chapter explores **why you're stuck**. We'll examine all the forces at play, turning the klieg light off cheaters for a moment and shining it squarely on chumps.

What gives us chumps our quintessential chumpiness? Spackle, hopium, and a dogged tenacity to untangle the skein of fuckupedness. (I'll explain all that in a moment.) After we master those concepts, I'll disassemble common chump fears one by one.

Untangling the Skein of Fuckupedness

Chumps spend a lot of time and energy trying to figure out cheaters. I call this dynamic "untangling the skein of fuckupedness."

Untangling the skein of fuckupedness is a coping mechanism. You want to figure out what makes your cheater tick so you can ensure that they never do anything so devastatingly hurtful again.

Of course, the skein is impossible to untangle, but by God, you're going to unknot it, piece by piece, make it linear and you **will** understand it!

Why do cheaters cheat? Greed, opportunity, and not caring as much as they should. Cheaters cheat because they can. Because they value ego kibbles more than they value your well-being.

Chumps often believe it is all *way more complicated* than that. We've got a vested interest in thinking greater forces are at work than just plain old entitlement. It's extremely painful to conclude that our cheaters have devalued us by choice. We don't matter? Ouch! So we frame their behavior as an *insight* problem—the cheater is compelled by unseen forces to behave this way! (Cheating is not a reflection of their values or who they really are.)

Chumps are great at devising theories to figure out their cheaters. Heck, cheaters don't even have to come up with an excuse as to "why"—we're usually right there supplying them with one.

> "I know this isn't the *real you*. I think you let your defenses down when your mother died, and it stirred up a lot of feelings about your self worth, and you were in a dark place and needed validation. Then Cheryl started coming on to you, that relentless bitch, and you let your boundaries down because you were broken, but it's all a mistake—a terrible mistake! Our love is bigger than this, right? *Right?*"

Cheaters are quite happy to let you untangle the skein of fuckupedness because that's energy directed at them. (Kibbles!) And it saves them from the onerous task of honest self-reflection. Most cheaters suck at self-reflection, shit-owning, and other forms of maturity. If they try to answer "why", they tend toward blameshifting and self-pity. Bad therapy helps a lot with this. With a disordered person, therapy is an opportunity to acquire a whole new vocabulary with which to mindfuck you.

> "Yes, I was in a dark place. And Cheryl was there for me in a way you couldn't be. You never did meet my emotional needs, so there was that void. I suppose you'll have to try harder now since I did this Bad Thing (which doesn't define me, so don't even go there, because I have toxic shame and if you trigger my toxic shame I might feel compelled to cheat again). I need reassurance that you can show me unconditional love through this, while we examine the dynamics we both contributed to, which led me to cheat on you."

If you're a chump, you won't find that kind of crazy psychobabble at all repellent. No, you'll just keep unspooling the skein. Asking yourself why they're this way, and how do they really feel about the affair(s) and you, and what was your part in it all.

If you're a chump you feel it is your job to help them with this insight thing. If it's their family of origin (FOO) issues, well, you'll call and make that counseling appointment for them. Not only will you make the counseling appointments, next you'll get out your magic marker and highlight all the relevant chapters in the affair books you bought for them on Amazon. They don't read? No worries. You'll download the podcasts.

Untangling the skein is codependent behavior. You're trying to control outcomes you really cannot control. You're taking ownership of crap that's not yours to own. An explanation is not a balm and it doesn't prevent scary things from reoccurring either. The only thing a cheater can do is **demonstrate** they have remorse through their **actions**. (Preferably a very generous divorce settlement. Failing that, a very generous post-nup.)

Cheating isn't an insight problem, it's a character problem. The fallacy of the skein is that if you could just untangle it, you'd have this roadmap showing where all the landmines are planted. Then, if you could just Avoid Those Things, all will be fine.

No, the scary reality is, you don't control this. **You just control you**. (I'm going to say that a lot. In fact, maybe I'll publish another book that just says, "You don't control this, you only control you" on every page. You could put it under your pillow at night and maybe through osmosis the message will float up and implant itself in your brain. It's that essential to un-chumping.)

Chumps, STOP untangling the skein of fuckupedness! Figuring out the cheater is energy directed at **them**, which is energy deflected away from **yourself**. You're asking the pointless question of why they are this way, instead of asking yourself the harder question of—why am I hanging around this jerk?

Getting lost in the cheater's skein prolongs your pain. Better to move toward acceptance. They did it because they could. They can't unring that bell (or unfuck that whore). When you feel the urge to untangle, redirect that impulse to yourself—is this relationship acceptable to me? You've got only one skein to untangle and it's *yours*.

Yeah, but what if my cheater is mentally ill?

You may think you can bypass the "Don't untangle the skein" advice because *your cheater is different*. Your cheater suffers from a real mental illness or midlife crisis or addiction. You may spend a lot of time untangling exactly what sort of affliction your cheater suffers from. Is he a sex addict? Does she have Narcissistic Personality Disorder? Is he a sociopath? Is she a Borderline?

Chumps, it's not for you to say. That's the call of an experienced mental health professional. But here's the deal—a lot of disordered people don't go to therapy willingly. They're dragged there by their ear. So don't expect a narcissist or sociopath to stick around for a proper evaluation. You may well be dealing with someone who is personality disordered. And chances are, unless you're fortunate to get the right sort of therapist who will see through their impression management, a therapist may be snowed too. At least in the short term.

My advice to you is—don't get deeply invested in your cheater's diagnosis, whether it's mental illness or sex addict or malignant narcissist. Put the focus back on yourself. You don't need to know what kind of flavor of fucked up it is to know it's fucked up. You know enough to know that this behavior is toxic and you need to distance yourself from it.

One thing that is helpful, however, if you're going to do an armchair shrink diagnosis (or better yet, you get an actual one), is it gives you a framework to understand this person's baffling behaviors. With some education about character and personality disorder, you will start to recognize the manipulations—and that is terrifically useful. It also helps you feel less alone. Other people struggle to have relationships with disordered people too. It helps to say this remorseless, callous behavior is "disordered" period, and not the normal sort of treatment you should accept.

One pitfall we chumps fall into, however, is that we think oh, if it has a **label**, we can get behind that and love all the hurt away. Sex addict? Hey, it's an illness, I need to be there for him and hold his hand through recovery. Bipolar? Hey, she can't help it and in sickness and health, right?

No, you matter too. Don't overestimate your powers—recovery from this kind of fucked up is best left to professionals who can be impartial. You're not impartial, you're invested. It's okay to save yourself from whatever manner of crazy it is. Please do.

If you want my opinion (a chump and not a mental health professional's) I don't think normal people can conduct double lives for any duration. To do that you have to have little to zero empathy, and such people are wired wrong. A few sandwiches shy of a picnic. Whack. Not marriage material, to say the very least. I think you have better things to do with your life than partner up with someone who may be congenitally incapable of loving you in a healthy way.

Spackle

Spackle is the miracle substance we use to cover the unsightly blemishes in our relationships. Spackle fills in the gaps and creates a smoother surface. Add a little sanding and paint—and voila! A normal looking surface!

After infidelity, it's not uncommon to feel like you never knew who your cheater was at all. You might feel like you loved a holographic projection of a loving spouse, but really some sicko was behind the projector. Or maybe you still cling to the idea that they were once a good person, but got abducted by aliens and replaced with an amoral jerk.

Who *was* this person and how could they have deceived me?

Well, maybe part of it was *you*. Maybe you spackled.

All relationships all possess some spackle to one degree or another. For instance, I look past my husband's penchant for "Polka Pimp" t-shirts and dressing like a teenage refugee. If anyone asks, I'll tell you he is the most handsome, wonderful husband on the planet, and not a flaming

dork. Conversely, when I enter the house, I take my shoes off in the most inconvenient traffic paths imaginable. I don't know why. No one can break me of this. It has driven everyone who has ever lived with me crazy. My father used to punt my shoes down the hallway or hide them from me. If you ask my husband, he'd tell you I'm a delight to live with. I know I'm not. I know that my shoe habit among other idiosyncrasies (snoring, complaining about Texas weather, organic food snobbery) make people want to strangle me, but my husband is nice and looks past my insufferable qualities.

A little spackle is kind. Necessary, if you want to remain happily married. Too much spackle, however, is dysfunctional—delusional even.

What does bad spackle look like? Making continual excuses for bad behavior. Creating a positive narrative from spotty evidence. Constructing "underlying issues" that explain destructive choices.

Spackle examples: He isn't really a cheater, he just has "bad coping mechanisms for stress." She isn't really a failure because she hasn't kept a steady job in 20 years, it's because she intimidates her bosses. They can't handle how clever she is and so they undermine her. He isn't a mooch. He has a lot of potential and is going to stay at home and write that screenplay for a few years.

Sparkly people (narcissists, Cluster Bs, whatever you want to call them) are really good at maintaining an air of being All That. They *so* believe it, that you do feel a little crazy around them if you don't believe it too. And face it, most of us *want* to believe that we chose the smartest, best looking, most fabulous person as our spouse. Because that reflects well on us. We spackle out of self-interest, as well as love.

The problem is that a lot of cheaters are frauds. They really wouldn't look normal to the outside world if anyone knew their true selves. We are there to spackle and smooth their image to the world. We are of use to them. We polish and finesse and build them up. We are so invested in that image, that we do this work gladly, sometimes unwittingly. If the cognitive dissonance between what is and what we want it to be is too great, then we stuff that down. Until there comes a point at which you can't pretend any more.

Infidelity is liberating in a sense, because the true person is revealed. You weren't going crazy. The emperor really didn't have any clothes. But damn it, if you weren't one of the idiots saying he did.

And why is that?

1. **We want to believe**. We have a vested interest in thinking our world is normal and safe and we chose a good spouse who reflects well upon us.

2. **They really do believe they're better, and so we buy it too**. Why would someone act smarter than me, if they didn't possess the accomplishments to go along with that air of superiority? Wow. They must *actually* be smarter and more deserving than me!

3. **We don't look at the evidence**. If you pay attention to actions and not lip service, it's pretty easy to spot who is sincere in our lives and who is a waste of space. But often those conclusions are painful to draw, and so we're sucked in by pretty words and attitude. We construct realities based on spackle and no substance.

As a chump, I have been guilty of spackle crimes. I constructed all sort of reasons why my cheating ex was really a good person deep down and not a freaking abusive wing nut. He had an "inferiority complex" for growing up poor. He had mommy issues. He had daddy issues. The problem was really the other woman, he needed to feel needed and she was just manipulating him! You name the delusional excuse, I had it.

Lesson learned: If you've got a little ding in your wall, spackle is good. But it's nothing to build the foundation of your house out of.

Hopium

Spackle is the gateway drug to hopium. When you can't spackle any longer, you have to hit the harder stuff—delusional hope or "hopium." It's a powerful hallucinogenic. Hopium can make you see potential in the grimmest set of circumstances.

How do you know when you're under the influence of hopium? You speak in terms of your cheater's **potential** and not the evidence. Wow, she could be a great partner… if only. Or—I want the guy I thought I married back. Wistful "woulda, coulda, shoulda" fantasies are a sign you're high on hopium. If you find yourself grasping at the smallest indication that this person gives a shit about you—you've got hope sickness.

It's hard to be down on hope. It's hard to fault people who are hopeful. It seems virtuous. But in cases of infidelity, it can keep you stuck. Listen to me betrayed people—**hope is not your friend**. You need to bludgeon hope with a fencepost and begin to operate with total lucidity.

Because hope is so strong, cheaters know exactly what a powerful manipulation tool this is. The goal of a cheater is **cake**. Your goal is to get them to come to their senses and be that sparkly person you fell in love with and commit to you. So they will use hope to keep you on the hook. They will feign remorse, cry, and say they miss you. They may go to counseling. Admit, hey, they aren't perfect or Mistakes Were Made. They may crack open a book (usually something like "When Splendid People Cheat.") And you, desperate to save this mess—take it as a Sign.

The only antidote to hope sickness is self-knowledge. Know what you will and will not tolerate. What your values are. Where your boundaries are. Be unswerving in your loyalty to your well-being and what sort of relationship you want. Hold out for that. Cheaters lie and they lie cleverly. So it is essential to **watch what your cheater does and pay zero attention to what they say**.

This is very hard to do. Hope is like that siren song in Ulysses. You're going to have to tie yourself to the mast and stuff cotton in your ears. But stay strong, because crazy hope that this person is going to fix this and stop hurting you—in the face of evidence to the contrary—is the number one reason why people stay stuck with cheaters.

Chump Fears

Hope and fear are the one-two punch that keeps chumps stuck. Why the hopium? The fear of what comes next.

I don't think it's wrong to be hopeful in the face of fear. As the saying goes, the opposite of fear is faith. I just happen to think hope pinned on cheaters is misplaced faith. It's much more productive to pin your hopes on yourself. If you're going to bet on anyone, bet on you. Bet on your resiliency and ability to create a better future for yourself—you get to control that. Controlling cheaters? Not so much.

But I won't minimize what a total clusterfuck infidelity is. You'd be an idiot if you weren't afraid of losing everything you hold dear—your family, your home, your financial future. Of course you're scared witless of what comes next. And of course you are protective of what you love. I don't think chumps just stay stuck out of fear alone—you can stay stuck out of bravery. Out of a deep tenacity to love in the face of pain, to rise above humiliation to save your marriage.

Chumps have big hearts, and that is a beautiful quality. One of the most heartbreaking realizations about chumpdom, however, is that **love is not enough**. Grown-up love is conditional love. Loving without deal breakers is not sustainable; it's an invitation to be abused. You cannot love someone into respecting you. Love isn't magic pixie dust. Tenaciously loving your cheater doesn't transform them into a better partner. It's misdirecting your noblest impulses and bestowing your gifts on someone who doesn't sufficiently appreciate them.

What would happen if you found your badass and loved yourself more than you love your cheater? What keeps you flinging kibbles into an endless black hole? What are you afraid of?

Let's take apart some common chumps fears:

I'm afraid divorce will hurt my children.

This is huge, because of course divorce does hurt children. And no loving parent wants to deliberately hurt their children. Cheaters may say, "Oh, children are resilient"—but they have absolutely no right to say that. Yes, children are resilient, but they never should've been put in this position by the cheater. It's a like a mugger pistol-whipping you and saying, "Hey, your face will heal." It will... but that's not the point.

"Staying for the children" keeps cheaters in cake. If the kids were so very important to them, why did they cheat in the first place and risk their intact home life? It puts you in a game of chicken, and they're counting on you flinching first. You love the kids, you'd never break up the family, and so you'll never impose that consequence of divorce. Ergo cake.

Imposing a divorce on your children because of your partner's infidelity is like one of those horrific civil wars where rebels force innocent villagers to kill their own family members. If you're married to a cake eater who won't stop cheating, you have to be the person to put the bullet in the marriage. You get to deliver the deathblow. The cake eater isn't going to do it. The injustice of that is shattering. Really? *You, the committed person?* You have to be the bad guy?

The cheater is the bad guy. Don't accept that role. Don't take responsibility for the fallout. By divorcing, you are just imposing the consequences that result from the cheater's selfish destructiveness. You are not being selfish—you are protecting yourself and your children from further harm. The reason cake eaters don't file for divorce (aside from the deliciousness of cake itself) is that they would prefer to pawn bad guy status off on you. They are simply sad sausages, who just needed more time, and who were *really trying*. But you! You're a *quitter*! A selfish person who doesn't consider the children!

Please be above such crazy talk. Just because they blameshift, doesn't mean you have to accept the blame. Mark that crap package "return to sender."

Also consider that staying married to a cheater "for the children" role models dysfunction. You're creating a future generation of chumps and cheaters, who will believe that disrespect, a lack of reciprocity, and emotional abuse (lying, gaslighting, blameshifting) are normal. Don't think kids don't internalize what's going on. You may imagine you're protecting them and discover they know a lot more than you think.

When you divorce a cheater you are modeling resiliency to your kids and a grown-up notion of what love is. When someone abuses you, there are consequences. It's not just okay to enforce boundaries, it's *essential* to protect yourself from further harm. People don't just nebulously "fall out of love"—life has deal breakers.

As a chump whose child has been through divorce, let me tell you this—children *are* resilient. And they take their clues from you. Show your kids what it is to rise to a challenge with dignity. Unfortunately, we cannot always shield our kids from pain. Life has its sucker punches and divorce is one of them. All you can do is set the best example you can and be the sane, responsible, consistent parent who loves them.

I like to say, children just need one sane parent. Some kids don't even get that. Obviously, you went into this thing thinking you'd get the gold standard—two sane parents and an intact family. A parent stuck in an affair, however, is not someone who is putting their family first, no matter how many spasms of Disney-like attention they muster up on occasion. So, sorry, the sane parent job falls to you.

Chances are you've been doing the responsible parent gig all along. You'll find it's much easier really to parent without a cheater and all their attendant drama. Attention that was once focused on the cheater can now be transferred to yourself and your kids. The peace is divine. Don't let anyone tell you single parenting means a "broken home." The only broken thing is the cheater. You are a ROCK. So listen, stop beating yourself up about single parenthood—your kids have an intact family—you and them. Now it's just minus one fucktard.

I'm afraid the affair partner will "win" if I let go.

What exactly is the affair partner "winning"? You're fighting over a sugar-coated dog turd here. Please let go and give Mr./Ms. Schmoopie the satisfaction of winning a dog turd. The frosting will slip off in time, I promise you. While a cheater is in an affair, they are heavily frosting their turd, trying to cover the stench, but their essential turd core remains.

Cheaters are not prizes to win. When you're in that mentality, you're doing the pick me dance. You need to ask yourself if you want a marriage that's an ongoing contest with at least three people in it.

But! But! They're going to be different for the affair partner! And you'll miss out! And you've invested so much to just walk away now!

Look, I'm sorry about your sunk costs, but put your mind at rest, your cheater is not going to be different for their affair partner. Cheaters don't have magical character transplants. They're still the same selfish person with crap life skills. Thinking they will be different for someone else is just another way of believing the infidelity has something to do with you. It doesn't. It not about whether or not the Other Woman has bigger tits or a trustfund, or the Other Man earns more money and has straighter teeth (chances are he's a troll)—it's about kibbles. Who is a better source of narcissistic supply? The answer to that is usually—both of you. Cake.

Nothing delights a cheater more than centrality. If your cheater has left for the affair partner, and you want to thwart their happiness—playing the obstacle *increases* their happiness. Not to mention it's keeping you from getting on with your own life. No, cheaters *love* a triangle (rectangle, hexagon, dodecahedron...) Acting like the cheater is a prize, makes the affair partner think they **won** a prize! It makes you the foil to their star-crossed love. It gives them shivers of delight to know how much you care.

Refuse to be a hypotenuse! So what if the affair partner thinks they "won"? They think all sorts of moronic things. You don't control that. Walk away from this dog turd in disgust. You're above this. Congratulate the affair partner on their good fortune winning a turd.

People who are remorseful do not put you in a position of competing for their love.

I'm afraid of the financial fall out.

Do you want a life or a lifestyle? Very few people divorce without a significant financial loss. I'm sorry, it's part of the shit sandwich of infidelity. But if your cheater is like many, they're not that trustworthy with their money either. It's not unusual to discover thousands of dollars spent on affairs or to experience other financial infidelity—chaotic spending habits, secret accounts, missing savings. You might be supporting your cheater financially and fear paying support indefinitely. If you stay, you might assume you could control the outcome, cajole them toward steady work, and reconsider leaving then.

Alternatively, you might be financially dependent on your cheater and postpone leaving until you can support yourself.

These are all issues to take up with an experienced family law lawyer. Don't make any assumptions about the finances of divorce until you get a professional opinion or two. If you're dependent, you can ask for alimony or temporary support. If you're supporting, you may be able to work out a deal in which you do a lump sum buyout.

But whatever you do, don't expect your situation to remain static. When you're aware of financial infidelity, expect more of the same. You are taking a risk by staying that is equal to or greater than leaving. While you wait, your cheater could be moving assets to leave *you*. Don't trust the status quo. Please game out your options.

Whatever you're left with after divorce, you'll find a great freedom in captaining your own ship. When you stay with someone who is financially unfaithful, it's like a game of whack-a-mole, reacting to one disturbing discovery after the next. Sure, you might be poorer after divorce, but you won't be living with a crazed prairie vole who is undermining you either.

When I had my D-Day, my cheater had just moved me to a new state. I was freelancing and suddenly had to find full-time employment. All of my money was tied up in a house I had just purchased with him, and I very stupidly had paid off $16,000 of his personal debt to get a better mortgage rate on the house. In other words, I had made all of my premarital assets marital assets—and I was fucked. He was a patent attorney who made six figures. I was a single mom, who found a job at a farming newspaper, and made $33,000 a year. (The worst paid job I'd had in 20 years and I was grateful to get it.)

When I left him I discovered that even on my tiny salary, I was happy and I made it work. I felt a huge amount of pride being the sole breadwinner. Was it humbling? Yes—I went down in jobs, gave up a giant house I sunk a ton of money into, and I had to borrow money off a friend until my divorce settlement came through—God bless her. But I did it.

Every day people write to me how they did it too, and under far more challenging circumstances. They go back to school, they move in with their parents, they sell off the family homestead. What they all have in common besides resiliency was the ability to respond to infidelity as a **crisis**.

You don't question the financial fall out when a tornado rips the roof off your house, do you? No, you just run for your life. You get to safety and then you figure out the particulars of what next.

Think of financial infidelity as a tornado. Listen to the sirens. Get help.

I'm afraid to be alone.

It's scary to leave someone. We humans are programmed to bond. Ever read about that famous Harlow study about baby monkeys? Some baby monkeys are put in a cage with real monkey mommies and some in a cage with barbed wire mommies, wrapped in a thin veneer of terry cloth—a pale mommy monkey substitute. But the babies with the barbed wire mommies try to bond with that thing. Even though they get pricked and are bleeding and the entire experience sucks. Inside their little baby monkey brains, they must be thinking... something better than this exists. But they haven't experienced it. So they cling hard to the barbed wire monkey. Of course, the babies with the real mommies are thriving.

Moral of the story? Step out of the cage and go find some real monkeys to bond with. It's scary to leave the barbed wire monkey—but if you find the courage to do it, you'll experience true monkeys. You don't know what you've been missing.

Don't waste your life on a barbed wire monkey.

I don't want to fail.

People get so hung up on the "failure" aspect of divorce, instead of asking themselves **at what cost am I keeping this together**? Is your health suffering? Are you a bucket of stress? Consider what you're missing out on by staying—like your ability to find another faithful partner some day.

I get it, it's hard to admit to yourself and the world that you fucked up something as important as choosing a life partner. Being cheated on is humiliating. It's natural to want to control the outcome. Either you don't tell anyone (and suffer alone or on online forums or in your therapist's office), or you tell people and spend the rest of your marriage either avoiding everyone who hates your cheating spouse or convincing them that your Marriage Is Stronger For It.

Remember—**infidelity is not your failure to own**. Do not borrow shame. It takes a lot of strength and character to navigate this shit. If you loved a lousy partner, okay, so what? You're human. You picked from the barbed wire monkey pile. Explore that, fix it, and choose better next time.

Maybe I'm exaggerating and it's not that bad.

Denial keeps chumps stuck. As coping mechanisms go, denial is pretty effective. Just be oblivious about your situation and your feelings about it. Poof! It never happened! We spackle over our life messes, because we're

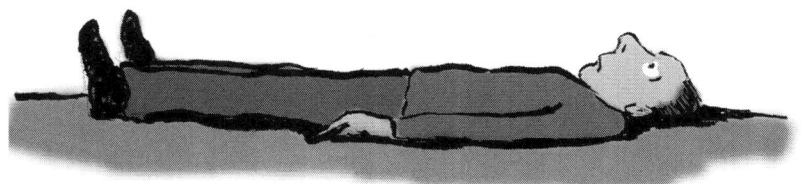

invested. It's hard to walk away from an investment, even a bad one. In fact, the more you invest, the harder it is to walk away, even when you know you're losing! Economists call the phenomena "sunk costs" and "loss aversion." So, naturally you just pretend the investment isn't really that bad.

If you want to get unstuck, you have to take a hard, unvarnished look at your reality.

You are entitled to your deal breakers—but for some people infidelity is not a deal breaker. It may be that those people reconcile and try to love their way into a different reality. Or it may be that some people just aren't that deep. Infidelity doesn't hurt if you're not that committed. I suppose to some superficial people, losing a partner is like swapping out an air filter or something.

But if you're a chump, you're rooted. You loved with your whole heart. You were completely invested in your shared life and infidelity is devastating. You might compare yourself to the un-invested, shallow people and wonder if you're making too much of a fuss about this. Chances are you might have a cheater that said as much. "Everyone cheats" or "Hey, Edith doesn't have a problem with it. Why can't you be more like Edith?" or some such.

You have to be true to your values. If you believe in monogamy and commitment—stand up for that! There's nothing wrong with you for expecting what you were promised. You're not naïve or unsophisticated—you were trusting.

It's completely normal to be grief stricken and angry. You were defrauded. It's ridiculous for a cheater to claim infidelity is "no big deal" because if they truly felt that way, they would not have kept it a secret. Cheaters keep their affairs hidden because they know it's wrong and they're trying to gain an unfair advantage (cake eating).

Minimizing infidelity is a directive to you to suck up your pain and accept disrespect. Don't accept that mindfuck.

I worry that this is the best I can do.

Nonsense. You could swing a cat and hit someone that's a better person than your cheater, just by virtue of the fact that person hasn't already cheated on you.

Trust that you deserve better. Trust that it isn't your lot in life to pick from the reject pile of humanity. Yes, we're all God's children and in some way flawed. This isn't about acceptance and unconditional love. Adult love comes with conditions—conditions like your partner should not act in ways to actively harm you. Conditions like mutuality and respect. Your cheater is not the be all and end all.

The best salesmen and charlatans excel at creating an air of exclusivity. *I have something very special to offer you. Are you elite enough to be worthy?* The cheater wants you to want them. They would love for you to do the humiliating dance of pick me and fight to be worthy. But face reality—your cheater betrayed you. They'd do anything for an ego kibble. *Anything.* They aren't exclusive. They're slutty.

There are other, much more deserving people out there than your cheater. People who won't make you tap dance for their love. Go find them!

Trust That They Suck

What spackle, hopium, and chump fears all have in common is **the disbelief that the cheater sucks**. *Surely there must be some way to preserve my good opinion of this person? How could I have been so duped?* This is the bargaining stage of grief. You're hoping to construct some narrative where you don't have to reconcile the person you loved with the horrible pain of betrayal.

Snap out of it. If you want to get unstuck, you have to start facing unpleasant realities. You must connect the dots between cheaters' words and actions and draw the painful conclusions. Don't give cheaters the benefit of the doubt—trust the evidence. Trust the omissions—the remorse that wasn't expressed, the no shows, and the trampled boundaries. Add it up. What does it tell you?

You are not responsible for being cheated on. That shit isn't your fault. **But you are entirely responsible for how you respond to abuse.** Chumps, that is on us.

Trust that they suck. And trust that you do not suck and deserve better.

CHAPTER 7

The Fine Art of No Contact

"Never miss a good chance to shut up."
—*Will Rogers*

The fastest track to healing after infidelity is no contact (NC). You have to shut off the flow of manipulation and kibble exchange. That means distancing yourself completely from the cheater. Obviously, this is much more difficult if you have children together (more on that in a minute). If you don't have children together, go cold turkey.

The problem with no contact is not the mechanics of it. No, the problem is mental. No contact is a **discipline**. It's resisting the urge to try to bargain and achieve consensus with the cheater. The "hows" of no contact are pretty straightforward. The "whys" of no contact are harder to grasp emotionally.

In the beginning, you'll find no contact excruciating. It's not just that you miss your cheater (or who you thought they were), it's that you'll fight the urge to tell them how you feel or demand that they explain themselves. You'll draft long, heartfelt emails and have to stop your twitchy "send" finger. You'll wonder why your phone isn't ringing and dread it when it does. You're going to be obsessive and overthink it all.

Going no contact is like kicking a drug. Take it minute-by-minute, hour-by-hour, day-by-day, week-by-week. The early days are the worst and you just have to tough out the delirium tremors. But the longer you go, the better you'll feel. You'll see the rewards, I promise.

Why Go No Contact?

For your sanity and protection. This is your way of gaining clarity and turning off the cheater mindfuck channel.

Chumps can often be disingenuous about no contact. It's taken up in a spirit of "Harrumph! Well, I'll show *you*!" And you think that your silence will goad your cheater into apologizing, or behaving, or showing you the proper deference and respect. This isn't trusting that they suck, folks. At the core of this behavior is hoping that your cheater will come back to you chastened. That's hopium. You don't stay no contact because you still want a relationship with them.

No contact is for you. It is the logical extension of trusting that they suck. There is nothing to say, no point in engaging. The jig is up. You understand who they really are and your silence speaks volumes.

Remember, if you want to end things with a narcissist, nothing says fuck off louder than silence. Disordered people **want** engagement. It's kibbles. They want a fight, or they want to hoover you and see if their charm still works on you. Don't give them the chance. Shields up, chumps.

If you've been married a long time, you're used to having this person to talk to, or bounce things off of. You thought the cheater was your friend, and you're having a hard time switching that part of your brain off. You still believe at some level that the cheater has your best interests at heart, and can be reasoned with. This is another "trust that they suck" issue.

Consider your values. Do you want to be friends with someone who cheats on you and shows you such little respect? And why would you think you could reason with someone who is a proven liar?

Get out of the habit of talking and arguing with them. Why would you believe a word they say? Everything you need to know is in their **actions**. If they're sorry, they will cooperate with a divorce. If they care about their children, they will pay support. If you have to beg for these things, there's your answer. There is no need to discuss anything, let the lawyers work it out. When a cheater's words do not align with their actions, it's impression management. They're trying to manipulate you.

Do you really want to eat the shit sandwich of pleasant small talk? Of this person acting like your friend, while draining your bank account, or suing you for custody, or spending your marital resources on their affair partner(s)?

Treat this person with all the courtesy you'd give your local county tax assessor. It's just business, chumps. And most business can be conducted by email. (Always err on the side of documentation any way.)

Do Not Feed the Beast

No contact deprives cheaters of kibbles. All attention is good attention. All kibbles are good kibbles. It's up to you to stop feeding the beast.

Cheating is manipulative behavior. Expect more of the same when you divorce a cheater. Engaging in long discussions, telling the cheater how you feel, and what you're going to do is giving them ammunition to manipulate you with.

Silence is self-protection. It's much harder to manipulate you if you don't give them the raw materials. Not only do you hide your buttons, no contact deprives them of kibbles and feelings of centrality. Which of course cheaters hate, so expect that they'll come fishing.

What does that look like? It might be antagonistic—goading, insulting, provocation. Or it might be charming—faux friendliness, seductiveness, assenting to

commitments they have no intention of honoring. Usually, it's just a big combo plate.

Chumps struggle to not react because they think they can reason a wing nut into consensus. They still think at some level they can manage this outcome. (Which is your own kind of chump control freakiness, really. Let that go.)

Let's say your cheater owes you child support. And you keep writing and calling and imploring them to do the honorable thing and pay for their children.

It's kibbles and power to the disordered person. They'll blow you off. They'll make fake promises. They'll deliberately frustrate you. You are an annoying buzzing sound. What they will enjoy, however, is fucking with your head.

But you the chump persevere. YOU WILL LISTEN TO ME! You'll get louder, more strident, more demanding. You might even threaten them with action.

Please skip all that and get straight to action. **Enforce your boundaries**. They don't pay child support? You call your lawyer. You get a court order. You deal with your local county child support enforcement agency. What you do **not** do is go through your cheater to get things done. They had that chance. Their actions told you their answer. Now you need to take care of this for **you**. No discussion necessary.

You can apply this to every other situation. They won't move their crap out of your garage? Sell it. Move it for them to a storage locker and send them the bill. They won't honor their debts? Small claims court. They won't visit their children? Don't expect them to. Quit twisting on a rope accommodating them.

Chumps don't enforce boundaries because we think the cheater's emotional state is **our responsibility**. But they're so sad! They're so angry! I must respond. I must prove I'm not the bad person they say I am. You've grown accustomed to your role as Soother-In-Chief. And Person Whose Fault It Always Is. STOP IT. Not your job anymore. Don't engage! Quit feeding the beast!

The difficulty of no contact is giving yourself permission NOT to engage. Walk away from the tasty bait the freak in your life keeps casting at you.

Learn to **say NO**. No, I do not have to accommodate your schedule. No, I do not have to comfort your distress. No, I do not have to defend my position to you.

In other words, allow yourself boundaries. Saying no does not make you an asshole. You know what makes you an asshole? Batter-ramming someone else's boundaries. If you've been with a freak, they feel very entitled to you accommodating them. They're used to you having zero boundaries where they are concerned. And when you got uppity before, they knew exactly how to put you back in your place—with guilt, or anger, or even charm. But now that isn't working for them any more. So when you try NC out on them, fully expect your freak to lose their shit. They will push those boundaries harder. Your job is to disengage.

This takes some practice, but I promise you will get the hang of it, and every time you do, it will feel a bit exhilarating. It's liberating to say no! Remember, when they cheated, they fired you from the job of caring about them.

How to Go No Contact When You Do Not Have Kids Together

Consider yourself fortunate if you don't have children with your cheater. You can have a surgically clean break. Change your number and block theirs. Unfriend them on social media. You don't need a portal into their life and they don't need one into yours.

Ensure that all communication goes through your lawyer and not to you directly. Enforce this boundary. There is nothing they need to say to you that cannot be said to your attorney. It's **over**, so the only thing left to discuss is logistics. Anything else—a relationship autopsy, an apology, recriminations—is a ploy to keep you engaged with them for cake. Logistical details about the storage unit or sale of the house? The lawyers can work that out.

Is this expensive? Yes. But nothing says firewall to your soon-to-be-ex like legal counsel. It's one thing to try and intimidate you or flatter you into a better settlement. It's quite another thing to try that shit on a member of the bar. The lawyers have seen it all. Please let your lawyer handle it and enjoy the peace of mind—and no contact—that you're getting for your money.

Unless you're dealing with a wing nut who represents themselves (pro se), there is a cost for the cheater too in fucking with you because they have to pay *their* attorney. Most disordered people may pester you for a while, but my experience is that it's not very satisfying for them. A) They don't get a reaction from you, just your attorney. Not as much fun. And B) Even wing nuts feel it in their pocketbooks. And that, sadly, is the most effective deterrent I know of. They won't quit harassing you because it's the right thing to do—they'll quit harassing you because there is a financial consequence to them for doing so.

How to Go No Contact When You Have Kids Together

When you have kids with a cheater, no contact is a Zen practice you'll have to master over years. You can go no contact on many fronts, just not all fronts. Your job is to learn to edit what those fronts are—children, schedules, and finances. And within those zones, you must learn to edit again, resist drama, and keep your responses brief and on target.

Remember, it takes two to psychodrama. Your cheater may try to pull you in, but that doesn't mean you have to respond. Employ strategies to help you maintain a respectful distance. Only communicate via email (because it's documentable). Use an online calendar to do scheduling and don't rely on verbal promises or texts. Divert all emails from them to a separate folder. If you get a disturbing email from your cheater, have a friend review it first. (You can always snark about it later.)

Keep all communication short and business-like.

Use the smallest sentence structure possible, and only discuss kid logistics, schedule, and finances. If they try to lead you down the rabbit hole of engagement—"That's why Taylor is flunking geometry—she inherited your math stupidity!"—don't go there. Reply, "Taylor will be ready for her visitation on Friday."

Don't ask them questions, if you can at all avoid it.

Don't ask, "Will you be taking Taylor this Friday?" Say instead, "Taylor will ready for her visitation on Friday" if Friday is the court-appointed day. Showing up is fucktard's responsibility. Fucktard doesn't show? You document that with another email. (The court system values documentation highly!) The ball must always be lobbed into their court.

Don't do their job for them.

It keeps you engaged with their idiocy, which opens the channels of crazy talk, as you plead and negotiate with them to Do The Right Thing. Remember this is centrality and kibbles, and they love that.

When you have kids, they have you by the curly short hairs. You will always want to throw yourself on a cheater's grenade of crazy to protect your kids. I'm not saying don't make reasonable accommodations to the schedule, (do it by email, business-like), I'm not saying be rude—no, as I've said before, regard them with all the politeness you reserve for you local county tax assessor.

But you mustn't pick up their slack if you can at all help it. If they've got a court ordered obligation to do something? Hold them to it. If they don't do it? Enforce consequences. Document all of it.

Remember, you don't control your cheater, you just control you. A lot of what you don't control is completely galling. How soon they introduce the affair partner to your kids. Lax parenting. What kind of crap they watch on television. But unless it rises to the level of danger to the children, the court won't care. Too many video games are not an immediate danger. Skanky girlfriend who bakes cupcakes and thinks your daughter is her new best friend is not immediate danger. Galling? Yes. Something a judge cares about? No.

I file these kinds of problems under "The unending punishment of breeding with a fucktard." They are the unavoidable shit sandwiches of co-parenting with a lousy person. If it rises to the level of serious harm—drug abuse, sexual abuse, physical abuse? **Absolutely do not hesitate to take legal action**. In most cases, however, you're just reacting to some loser who wants all the control of a parent and none of the responsibility. I'm sorry. It sucks. They suck.

How to Go No Contact with a Scary Wing Nut

If your cheater persists in making unwelcome contact, if they show up at your workplace or home, if they enlist third parties to contact you on their behalf—have your lawyer send the cheater an official no contact letter as the first step to filing criminal harassment charges. Have their workplace and local law enforcement cc-ed as well.

If your cheater threatens you in any way (verbal threats are just as illegal as physical ones) **go immediately to law enforcement** and get a protection from abuse order. Initially this order will be temporary until a permanent order can be filed. Talk to a domestic abuse hotline for professional support. Free counseling and legal support are often provided in situations like this. Please, please, PLEASE reach out to professionals.

I've been in this situation, and I know exactly how scary and mortifying it is, but you must protect yourself. A person who would violate your boundaries this flagrantly and threaten you is disordered and dangerous. Don't take your chances—take every precaution. Abuse escalates when you leave.

If your cheater violates a temporary or permanent protection order by still making contact, call 911. This is cause for arrest. Wing nuts will often test your resolve. Do not soften your boundaries, or drop the order, or take them back. I guarantee they will build the walls higher to make it harder for you to break out next time.

If you fumble, find your resolve and get another order. Don't worry that you won't be believed. Professionals see this all the time. It takes a woman an average of **seven** protection orders to leave an abuser. Please improve those odds and leave after one. Don't muddy the waters by taking an abuser back and getting sucked into the cycle. No "honeymoon" phase is worth the hell that follows.

Men, if your cheater is disordered, you may be wrongfully accused of abuse. If it's legal in your state, consider carrying a voice-activated recorder and do not allow yourself to be alone with this person.

Normal, healthy, remorseful people do not annihilate your boundaries. **Only freaks**. There is nothing here to save—NC all the way.

The Beauty of No Contact

When you're toughing it out on NC, keep your eyes on the prize—your healing. No contact means you are not giving this person the opportunity to hurt you any longer. You are shutting their shit down. You are refusing to be a dispenser of kibbles, no longer accepting the blameshifting, and are refusing to be of use to them.

In short, you're asserting your boundaries and taking back your power. Keep at it!

After you've maintained no contact for a while, you'll notice the spell is breaking. You feel like your better self again. You'll enjoy the peace and not reacting to the cheater's drama. You might feel twinges of guilt about that (shouldn't I care about their drama?) You might, like a bad drug high, kind of miss the drama. (Surely the drama means they *really care about me*, and that's why it's all so… dramatic?) But stay the course. In six months to a year, you'll be mortified that you ever knew this person and were their chump. Years out, it will feel like someone else's bad dream. That was my life?

What happens with life minus one cheating fucktard? You. You happen.

Chapter 8

What Was Real? Does It Matter?

> *"The more complete the despotism, the more smoothly all things move on the surface."*
> —*Elizabeth Cady Stanton*

Infidelity is the theft of your reality. People don't understand that unless it's happened to them. It's a most intimate kind of abuse. If someone mugs you, as frightening as that is, you know it's nothing personal. The mugger just wanted the money in your wallet and didn't care if you got hurt. Predator. Prey. It's a simply understood exchange.

Infidelity is uglier.

The victim of infidelity lives a lie of assumed safety with the person they love. The lie goes on for months or years, maybe even decades. But unlike the mugging victim, the infidelity victim *gives freely*. They're not held up at gunpoint. No, they generously give their wallet, their sex life, their career, their children, their time —every resource they have at their disposal goes to the cheater. It's a much more insidious theft. And the theft is possible only because we've been duped into believing this person loves us and is on our team.

Cheaters make unilateral decisions about their victim's health and welfare. And they act in secret, because chumps have value to them— value they want to continue extracting. Chumps can waste years in a marriage not knowing the truth about being defrauded. So much of our culture wants us to think these costs are frivolous. Infidelity is the jolly subject of romantic comedies or breezy women's magazine articles about the naughty fun of being a mistress. Wink, wink, nudge, nudge. Victimless crime!

No, it's shit like losing a pregnancy because you didn't know you caught a STD off your cheater. It's having to paternity test your children. It's herpes, HPV, HIV, and everything else they've got in the petri dish over at Planned Parenthood. It's your 12-year-old opening dad's laptop and finding pictures of dad fucking another woman that's not mom. It's the money missing from your accounts that went to pay for affairs, or worse—hookers.

Think I'm overstating it? None of those things happened to you? **They were risked**. And no one asked you if it was okay with you.

But that's just the collateral damage—diseases, hurt kids, and ruined finances.

The greatest indignity—the biggest mindfuck? Is that you **lose your story**.

You thought you were cherished. Special. Chosen. Committed. You thought you were a partner, husband, provider, father, confidant, wife, mother, family person. You thought you were a couple, part of a larger family, a fixture in your community.

And then you discover that everything you invested in was a lie. That wasn't your identity. Your identity was CHUMP.

Once you know you've been betrayed, you can't un-know it. Every memory is tainted or suspect. That Christmas, when we were opening presents with the kids? *You were texting him then?* When I was studying for that exam and you were going to give me time alone, you were really *with her?*

What was real? What was a lie?

Chumps torture themselves questioning their lives' narratives. *Were you happy then or was it an act? I thought she loved me, but clearly her mind was somewhere else. How could our relationship not matter? How could our children not matter? How could every year we spent together/time I cared for your mother/helped you when you were unemployed/nursed you through stomach flu/remembered your birthday NOT REGISTER?* **Why were you not bonded to me the way I was bonded to you?**

You rack your brain trying to sort out the moments that they Really Loved Me from the times they did not. You try to pinpoint when it all went bad. Often, you had no idea it was bad at all. The cheater seemed bonded. Okay, maybe not always, but normal life has it stresses and—well, HOW WAS I SUPPOSED TO KNOW?

You weren't. That's the mindfuck of it. Your reality was deliberately kept from you. You were played for a chump.

You cannot cheat on someone without gaslighting and lying to them, denying their reality, bit-by-bit, lie-by-lie. Stifling their suspicions, turning it back on them, accusing them of being crazy and over sensitive. Infidelity subverts chumps' sense of normalcy and makes them question the solidity of **everything**. *Who knew? Why didn't they tell me? Did my in-laws know? Have my friends welcomed this person into their circle? Did my kids know? Were they introduced to the affair partner? Is every single fucking thing in my life polluted?*

You know your bedroom is fucked up, if not fucked in. There is, of course, the sexual humiliation of infidelity. Your most intimate world has been violated. Perhaps your cheater ridiculed your sex life with their affair partner. Most likely you were not considered at all. You marvel at your invisibility, how inconsequential your connection was. The person you loved, whose body you mapped and knew every inch of is a total stranger. Moreover, you're a stranger to yourself.

Wasn't I special? Wasn't I loved?

Here's another kick to the gut—the very notion that you ever thought yourself special is used against you. How naïve of you to assume commitment. You don't own them. Everyone cheats. Monogamy is not natural. Why are you making such a big deal of this?

Cheaters will minimize and blameshift. Did I betray you? Well, I only did it because you were so inadequate/such a hard ass/sexless/impossible to live with/disdainful of my happiness. I never thought you'd know. It didn't mean anything. It meant everything. Goodbye. Don't leave me.

(After discovery, cheaters aren't really certain what you mean to them either, but they do know you're of use, and they'd prefer if you not tell anybody about this issue that is no big deal.)

People outside your life may point and question—how awful were you to make this person cheat on you? What were you lacking? Do you suck at sex? Clearly, you're clueless. How stupid you were not to see that you're a chump. Maybe you were in on it, had an "arrangement." This is your fault. How absurd you were to think you had a story, a place in the firmament of belonging.

The disconnect of betrayal, between the life you thought you had and the one you actually were living, is indescribably painful. People kill over it.

When you look back at the period of your life in which you were chumped, it's hard to know where to put that particular clusterfuck in the narrative. What was my real history? What was a sham? Does it even matter?

I spent a long time brooding on this. It was like my former marriage was a giant shit stew, and I was trying to fish out this little dumpling of actual "good times" and that little dumpling of "he loved me then"—until I realized—NO! Shit stew is inedible! You can't fish the dumplings out—they're swimming in shit!

Other people may have different stew-to-dumplings ratios, depending on the length of marriage, but chumps, my point is—this is a useless exercise.

To anyone reading this—I wish to God I could take your pain away. I wish I could restore your investment. Give you the golden 50-year anniversary you deserve, the legacy of an unbroken family. I wish I could give you back every wasted opportunity and every lost year. I once read that the playwright Tennessee Williams subtracted four years from his age for the four years he spent working in a shoe factory. I wish I could subtract your shoe factory.

But you don't get your old story back. To do that, you'd have to untangle the cheater's skein of fuckupedness—an impossible task that would keep you hopelessly focused on the cheater. But the good news is you can untangle yourself. You can pull the thread of **you** out from that gnarled mess.

Was my cheater a fake? A con artist? Did he love me, or whatever approximates love to such a person? I have no idea. I had to simply conclude that **I was real**. And in the end, that's the only person I control—me.

I brought my A game. I committed to that marriage. I tried to work it out. I was truly happy on my wedding day. I meant my vows. I enjoyed the fine May weather. The love of my friends and family. I enjoyed the catering, the flowers, and the iTunes dance mix.

That grinning, chumpy woman you see in her wedding pictures, who paid the bar tab for one of the other women, and assorted other wedding guests who knew of his cheating? In that moment, she was happy. That naïve woman on her honeymoon in Paris? She enjoyed the trip. That's who she was then. That **is** the story.

When it was happening, with all the evidence she had before her—she had every reason to be hopeful and optimistic. What came months later—the truth of who he was—doesn't change her.

This is what I learned about that narrative—I don't need his story to tell **my** story. I'll never know all of what was going on and with whom. I know enough to know it's disordered and dreadful and has everything to do with him, and nothing to do with me. I wasn't living a lie. **He** was living a lie.

There was a time when I thought the pain of infidelity would kill me. It didn't kill me. It made me appreciate opportunity. I moved on. I fell in love again. I found "meh." Paradoxically, none of the blessings I enjoy today would have happened if I didn't go through that nightmare. Doesn't make the nightmare okay, or my cheater any less of a freak. But had I not divorced a cheater, I would've never gotten tipsy in New Orleans and fallen in love with my husband, or written a blog, or left the safe confines of my reordered life.

We don't get the lives we expect, but ultimately that's okay. If you maintain your integrity, you get an authentic life, which is more than your cheater can say. There is no shame in loving with your whole heart, or counting on promises made to you. Good people invest when they love and they invest deeply. Just because someone tried to fuck with your reality doesn't mean they succeeded in actually altering reality. You're still you. This is still your story. You had a Potemkin partner, but it doesn't mean that plastic cutout person fronting a lie is any reflection on the solidity of you.

Was it real? **You're real**. Does it matter? **You matter**.

Know your worth. People who love with their whole hearts are gems. I'm sorry that cheating piece of shit didn't appreciate you. All we take forward from infidelity is what we learned from it, and when you survive, that's makes for a damn fine story.

CHAPTER 9

Getting to Meh

> *"It is only through labor and painful effort, by grim energy and resolute courage, that we move on to better things."*
> —Theodore Roosevelt

People often write to me and ask, "When is the pain going to stop?" and I reply "on Tuesday."

I don't know which Tuesday it will be, I only know that Tuesday is out there waiting for you.

Believe it or not, there comes a day when you don't feel the need for the karma bus to run over your cheater. You don't love them any longer, and you don't hate them. You just feel "meh."

Meh is not an acronym, although you could come up with some pretty nifty ones. "Must Exit Hell," or in "Memoriam Ex-Husband," or "Mother-Effing Hotdish!" Meh is just a bit of slang the cool kids use that means indifference, to not be bothered by. Meh also has a smattering of withering disdain. "You don't impress me. Whatever."

For chumps, **meh is the liberating state of acceptance**. On my blog, we chart our course by how close to meh we feel. Oops! Fell off the wagon, fed them some kibbles, got upset, "lost my meh."

Meh is what happens after you internalize "trust that they suck." You give up the drama, you give up trying to fix the cheater, or making them see the error of their ways. You just move on.

And when that annoying somebody crosses your path? They don't move you. At most, you might work yourself up to exasperation. *What is the point in trifling with this person?*

Meh is also a very pleasant state, because it stands in stark contrast to the previous drama. Oh, the crazy ride? I lost my ticket. Huh, guess I'll take this nice walk in the autumn woods instead.

Meh does not mean you don't find what they did utterly reprehensible. Rather, it's accepting that yes, this happened to me. And yes, this is who this person **really is**. You stop bargaining, you stop the "what ifs," you stop fishing around in the stew for Those Nice Qualities, trying to weigh them against infidelity and abandonment. Meh is putting the focus back on yourself, and your healing. Your new life eclipses your old life.

When this person just stops having the power to hurt you? That's meh.

Keep the faith that your Tuesday is out there. Some days it's a mental battle to slog through the pain. To make yourself walk the dog, or change the sheets, or finish your progress reports. To not let the injustice paralyze you. To tell yourself again and again "this person sucks" until you believe it. To live your life without the promise of justice. To just get on with things.

But one Tuesday, you will wake up and feel free. Oh thank God that is over. Whatever was I thinking to give so much of myself to so unworthy a person?

Fuck meh. I want revenge.

Oh save it for Oprah, Tracy. Shut up about this mythical "meh." I want to gut my cheater with a fish knife.

So you'd prefer revenge, huh? Some cosmic acknowledgment of your pain? Let's see that motherfucker choke on some of the humiliation for once?

I don't fault your feelings. Revenge is primal. When infidelity happened to me, I found myself channeling Chuck Norris. Suddenly, I was prone to the most gruesome revenge fantasies. My fat, hairy cheater would lay there asleep, snoring into his pillow, and I'd imagine what he'd look like disemboweled. Or with his head bashed in. Or pushed off a three-story ladder. These thoughts didn't even *disturb* me.

And here's the lunacy of infidelity—I felt that and I still tried to reconcile with him. My emotions went from—I want to KILL you! Don't leave me. Did I do something wrong? How COULD YOU?! I HATE your GUTS. Get OUT!—to—I feel nothing. I feel numb. I don't care what you do.

And when I thought of leaving him, all I could imagine was this Super Fabulous Glamorous Romance he was going to have with the other woman. I saw it as they would win and I would lose.

It took too long for it to dawn on me that I'd be much, much happier without this idiot in my life whom I frequently wished dead.

Besides a strong streak of self-preservation, I'm too sensible to push someone off a ladder. But I do not fault the urge. What I did with all that rage and injustice is—I let it fuel me toward a new life.

I didn't want the new life at first. I was miserable that I was going have to reinvent myself all over again. But in moving forward, and rebuilding my life, I learned a few lessons about revenge. They may not seem as satisfying as a violent, karmic reckoning, but they register and reverberate in the cheater's life—and are a lot more healing for you.

You want revenge? Here's how you do it:

1. **Practice "meh."** The cruelest thing you can do to a cheater is pay no attention to them. Their little narcissist souls die every time a kibble is lost. When you engage in

drama, you're filling their trough with ego kibbles. If you show them your pain the only thing that registers with them is that **they matter**. They feel central! Pretty! Fought over! When you practice indifference, however, it unnerves them. They usually try to up their kibble game with "remorse," or more in-your-face antics to get a rise from you. (Feed me! Feed me!) Do not give in. Practice "meh."

Remember, if you do something dumb but satisfying—I know a guy that sent the other man a giant bouquet of roses for Valentine's Day with an colorful Hallmark fuck off—all you do is solidify the cheater's narrative that you are batshit crazy and jealous. When you *don't* do that? Worse, if you're all classy and business-like? The narrative can't stick. They hate that.

2. **Let them live with the natural consequences of their shittiness**. Karma is just consequences. So step out of karma's way. Cheaters dodge responsibility. They pin the blame on you. They triangulate. But when you excuse yourself from their crazy, they have to live with themselves.

Divorce, of course, sucks. With the financial hits and the mortification factor. But more than that, cheaters have to either live with the crappy prize that is an affair partner, or go to the considerable trouble of finding a new sucker. It gets harder, especially when you aren't there to clean up their messes, pay the mortgage, and remember their mother's birthday for them.

You might have to wait years for them to nosedive, but they will. These are people who have crap life skills. The older they get, the less they sparkle. It becomes harder to operate on pure entitlement. And it just catches up with them, the debt, the lack of investment in relationships, the booze. Whatever it is, chances are they aren't going to wise up, get healthy, and face it. They'll use their same old crappy manipulations… with crappy results. Only you won't be around to pin it on. Their soul mate schmoopie gets that honor.

3. **Succeed**. As Frank Sinatra said, "The best revenge is massive success." Go be awesome. You'll enjoy that in its own right, but I promise you, it will get back to the cheater. "Frank lost 20 pounds, got promoted, and hiked across Nepal?" That nobody they thought you were, the dupe they

could cheat on, *you've* got game? It will eat at their guts. Indulge in the glory that your life is sweeter without them—and that they know it.

Listen, you don't need to whack your cheater with a threaded pipe, karma's got this. To butcher the words of Dr. Martin Luther King, "The arc of the universe is long, but it bends toward living in their mother's basement."

I'll never trust again.

Okay, perhaps you're past wanting to kill your cheater, but now everyone else is suspect. The other question I'm asked, second only to "When does the pain stop?" is "How will I ever trust again?"

You'll manage, but after infidelity, you should be a lot more discriminating and that's not a bad thing.

To say you must trust again may come across as flippant, or minimizing the trauma of betrayal. That's what's so insidious about infidelity—the total investment of it. I suppose infidelity doesn't hurt if you aren't that invested, if your connections are shallow. Sure, then you get over it. The wounds are superficial.

But if you're rooted, if you love with your whole heart, and your family means the world to you—the theft of that life is devastating. Because it's not just that the earth opened up and swallowed up everything you hold dear, like some natural disaster, no—some idiot did this to you. Because you didn't matter to them. Because they weren't invested. Because it was easier to lie to you and extract value from you, and let you go on believing your world was safe when it wasn't.

Betrayal is shattering. Coming back from it is just a series of small acts of bravery, one after the next, as you piece your world back together again. How far you go rebuilding is really up to you.

Some folks might get stuck at the trauma stage of "I'll never trust again"—and to me, that's terribly sad and incredibly impractical. *And I don't believe you.* Of course you'll trust again! You trust every day, if you didn't you'd be huddled in a bunker, agoraphobic, refusing to engage with the world. Trust is the social glue that holds us all together. You trust that the money you bought your latte with wasn't counterfeit. You trust your barista will not poison you. You trust a pilot every time you get on an airplane. You trust in democracy every time you elect an official and the world doesn't dissolve into anarchy and executions.

Every day we trust people and institutions, and don't think twice about it. We know intellectually that planes crash on occasion, and people get robbed, and institutions fail in far off lands and result in civil wars. But that doesn't stop us from traveling, or carrying money, or assuming democracy is safe. We'd like to think if some calamity were about to befall us, we'd get a warning. To the best of our ability, we manage risk. We don't walk in shady neighborhoods with $100 bills stuffed in our pockets. If peaceful democracy failed, we'd like to think we'd immigrate to Canada in time. We do the best we can. We trust in the overall solidness of our world.

And yet, intellectually we know that sometimes we don't get warnings. Innocent people get trapped in civil wars, people are mugged in broad daylight, mechanical failures cause planes to crash. We accept that the world has risks and that life can be cruel and unfair.

But we still live in the world, don't we? We still go on and engage with the world, don't we?

Learning to trust again after infidelity is a process of risk management and mostly just trusting yourself. Not trusting that you'll sniff out fraudsters with foolproof accuracy, but trusting that you're resilient and know how to face adversity.

I have to say, of all the infidelity fall out that I don't get, it's not trusting again.

Look, maybe I'm an epic chump, and a band of gypsies could carry me off in a sack, or offer to pave my driveway and take the money and never show up. Maybe it's pretty easy to roll me, but I don't want to live without trust.

Like you, I have every reason not to trust again when it comes to relationships. I'm a two-time loser. In my first marriage I was horrifically chumpy. I divorced a man with mental illness, paid him a shitload of money to retain custody of my son, and then he sued me for the next decade, mostly pro se. If that doesn't put you off love and marriage, I don't know what will—go live in the bowels of family court in Fairfax, Virginia. I estimate I lost about $100,000 in legal expenses. Does my head want to explode when I think about that? Yes, so I try not to think about it. Instead I focus on the fact that I survived it and my kid is great. What continues to piss me off is what a lousy father that guy is to my kid, but oh well. That's on him. No one misses him. His loss.

Anyway, I went through that freak show, was a single mom in my 30s, noodling around quite happy otherwise, when my path crossed with a serial cheater's. I'd like to think after my first divorce I had a better picker and knew how to enforce my boundaries better, or what the red flags of cheating look like. But I didn't when I was 37. I had no idea. I was a trusting chump—and when I invested in that relationship—I was **all** in. I totally committed, not halfway, but all the way. I moved with the cheater to another state, bought a house with him, had a custody trial to move my son. Gave up 16 years of friends and work in Washington, D.C. I loved with my big, huge chumpy heart.

And I got played. Totally sucker punched. Six months into my marriage his long-term mistress called. Then it was a series of incredibly stupid and heart-breaking false reconciliations. (Chumpy hearts die hard.)

Yeah, so my point is—I know what it is to lose. Hell, I know what it is to lose, try again and lose more.

But you know, I don't think I'd have it any other way. If you're going to love—**COMMIT**. Jump in with both feet. The whole thing was a horror show, but even the worst thing I ever did—marry that cheating idiot—led to some incredible blessings—living in beautiful Lancaster, Pennsylvania, wonderful friendships, a job I loved. Putting myself in that place was ultimately good for me.

The cheater was **not** good for me. And so I extracted myself—and it was painful as hell, and everything I learned about being betrayed I share with you here. I grew. I'm not the chump I used to be. I lost a fundamental innocence.

But I did not lose my ability to trust. Because, goddamn if I didn't love again! If you'd talked to me after my last divorce and told me I would move *again* for a man—oh, and he'd be another lawyer—oh, and it would be full of risk, oh, and it would be to the state of *Texas*? I would've told you to put down the crack pipe.

I love my husband. I always felt safe with him. But more than that, I learned a shitload from my two horrible marriages that preceded. Mostly, I learned to draw boundaries and enforce boundaries. I learned that I don't control most things, but I do get to control myself. And the pain and loneliness from those divorces made me appreciate opportunity. I was hungry to live to the fullest. I was sick of drama and unhappiness.

Pain and loneliness can make you go either way—close up in on yourself and tune the world out. Or it can make you reassess yourself. Examine your chumpy ways and change them. Preserve the best parts of character (the ability to love and commit) and jettison the not-so-great parts (spackle, denial, dependency, general idiocy.)

Life after chumpdom can also make you a bold risk taker. There is a freedom in losing everything and knowing that you survived. Bring it on universe! I've faced worse. This sentiment will liberate you. So when an opportunity presents itself to love and be loved? You say YES.

Next time around, I wasn't impetuous or foolish. No, I judged my husband's character to the best of my ability. I knew what red flags were, and I looked hard for them. I trusted my gut. We both have pre-nups. But it was still a risk. A big life risk. And you don't get the rewards of life without the taking risks.

So far, my risk has paid off—he's wonderful. But who knows—maybe he'll change. Maybe he'll broadside me. Or maybe life will sucker punch me some other way. Maybe one of us will get ill, have some horrible financial set back. Maybe all three kids will move into our basement at once.

Here's what's different—I speak up now. I draw boundaries. I enforce boundaries. Shit sandwiches are not a basic part of my diet any longer. In other words, I trust myself to handle what is thrown at me. I trust my resiliency. Why? Because it was forged in a goddamn blast furnace of psychodrama. I know I can rebuild and reinvent because I've had to do it over and over and over again. I accepted the painful growth that came from my mistakes, and from the shit that was inflicted on me unjustly.

I trust myself and I still trust others. Only one idiot betrayed me. He's an outlier. For one of him, there were dozens others who held me up, who helped me regain my life. I trust those people and I know they're good. There were hundreds of people on online forums, fellow chumps, who paid it forward for me—who took time out of their life to send me messages of support, to advise, to commiserate. Those total strangers cared about me.

Don't they outweigh the evil of one cheating fucktard?

Oh, but he's not the only one, you say! The world is full of cheating fucktards!

Yes it is. It's also full of good people, and it's full of chumps overcoming the damage cheating fucktards do, one brave act at a time.

So start small, folks. You can't trust anyone? That tells me you made your world too small. Specifically, you made your cheater your whole world. It's time to broaden your horizons and fill your life with good people who deserve you. How do you spot them? Well, some of them have always been there and others you'll have to cultivate. You do that by opening yourself to them, and being brave.

Let me ask you something—How would you feel if no one trusted you? Are you a good person? Are you trustworthy? How would you feel if I said you were a figment. You don't exist! Should I believe in **you**? How would you feel if I never knew your gifts? I never let myself trust you? We could never be friends because I assume the worst in you.

I'd be seriously missing out. Because you exist—thousands of you exist if my blog numbers are anything to go by.

Do your due diligence of course, but don't assume the worst in everyone or you're going to miss out on life's gifts. You don't have to partner up again if you don't want to. Maybe that's more risk than you care to assume. Maybe you're a cyclops and you're right, no one will ever love you. (Unless you date at CyclopsMatch.com.)

But for the love of God, let **someone** into your heart, okay? Be a friend, make a friend. When people demonstrate they aren't worthy—fire them. Be discerning, but be open to life.

Cheaters rob so much from us. Don't let them take your best self from you, that person who connects and feels intimate with others. They were idiots. They didn't have that ability to love with their whole hearts and commit to anything. You do have that ability—so why waste it? I'm not saying you have to lavish your love on another partner—but maybe you will, so don't rule it out. You don't know the future. Maybe you're going to lavish it on AIDs orphans or historical preservation societies or growing peonies. I have no clue what your personal happiness looks like.

But I know this—your happiness isn't with your cheater. That person is out of your life. Do not give them one more piece of your soul. Don't let

them win. They'd like nothing better for you to wither up and die from their rejection. Imagine if they were the last person you ever loved! How powerful they'd be! How you couldn't move on!

Do you want **that** to be your legacy?

How about you trust yourself to rise above one fucktard's opinion of your worth? How about you're awesome without them? How about you go **love, love, love** a million things that aren't them?

So get over it.

Yes, me, Chump Lady. I'm telling you that. Chump to chump. Get over it.

I know those are the three words every chump hates to hear. "Get over it," says your remorseless cheater after a half-assed attempt at reconciliation. "Get over it," says the friend who cannot conceive of your pain, and wishes you would just go back to your pleasant, ignorant self again. "Get over it," says your boss, because the drama is effecting your productivity.

I know "get over it" feels like insult to injury. A casual response to betrayal, the worst sort of minimizing. *So sorry I'm not healing at your convenience, asshole.* Chumps at once see the hidden agenda. The cheater who's not truly sorry. The friend who feels threatened by your vulnerability. The boss who doesn't really care, just get back to your widgets. So, quite rightly, chumps dismiss "get over it." Fuck you, I'll "get over it" when I'm good and ready. Perhaps not ever. I may go down with this ship if I fucking feel like it. Don't you tell **me** to "get over it"!

Get over it.

The pain is finite. Don't choose it. Don't keep reliving it. Infidelity does not define you. It's no measure of your soul, of your worthiness and lovability.

What keeps you in pain? Staying focused on your cheater. Their judgments of you, what makes them tick, who they're with now, what they're doing—and when the hell is the karma bus coming? Where is the karma timetable? I've been standing at this stop for years waiting for that bus. I demand a schedule! Only after that bus arrives will I be able to leave this stop and get on with my life properly! Damn bus.

Note the word **stop**. That's what happens when you wait for karma. Your life stops. You live a limbo of anticipation. Your focus is on the bus.

Stand on a different street corner and grab a different bus, chumps. One that's headed in the direction of your new cheater-free life. Focus on yourself.

Hell **yes** your job is to get over it! Reclaim your selfhood. Of course, it's a battle at times, but every liberation campaign is.

Getting over it is not eating a shit sandwich. You're not denying that this happened to you and it was abusive. You should not be friends with this person. Personally, I wouldn't touch them with a ten-foot barge pole. But you don't have to hold on to that righteous anger to know that their infidelity was real. It **was** real. It **did** happen. That person **sucks**.

Getting over it means they didn't break you.

You're not going to get over it staying married to a remorseless cheater. You get over it when you start to protect yourself, when you stand up and say "no more." When you draw those boundaries and enforce those boundaries. When you grieve. When you stop spackling and see the cheater for who they really are. When you let go of what you thought your life was going to be or should've been, and become open to the possibility of a new life.

Reconciliation is fine if you just want to survive. To limp along. To endure. I'm not convinced anyone every really gets over it when they stay married to a cheater. Seems like an endless buffet of shit sandwiches if you ask me.

I'd like to hold out a better vision for you. You're not just going to survive this—you're going to **thrive**. This is the painful birth to better days. This is where you discover exactly how badass you are. You find that job, you parent your way, you finish that degree, you fall in love again, you make new friends who get you, you create time for the old friends, you adopt an orphan, you get reacquainted with your creativity, you weld, you breed heritage cattle, you travel to Tibet, you start the lawnmower alone, you pass the bar, you own your successes.

What are the dimensions of that cheater-sized hole that's missing from your life? Every kibble you threw at narcissist's ungrateful ego—those belong to you now. Fill up your new life. Go give your love and talents to those deserving of you.

So you got to the last paragraph and I already told you how it was all going to end—you're going survive infidelity. Will you wear the scars? Yeah, but you'll wear them well. You're going to get over this, I have every confidence in you. Besides, what is there to miss exactly? The betrayal? Being treated like a concession prize? The disrespect? The pick me dance? The humiliation? *Oh, I'm going to hold those things close. Gee, I really want all that crap in my life.* No, of course you don't.

Grieve. Get over it. Tuesday is waiting for you.

About the Author

Tracy Schorn is a blogger, journalist, and cartoonist who lives in the barbecue capital of Texas with her husband, a civil rights lawyer, her teenage son, and two dogs with entitlement issues.

As a former chump, she'd like everyone to know—it gets better.